greatest ever

low carb

p

This is a Parragon Publishing Book
First published in 2004

Parragon Publishing
Queen Street House
4 Queen Street
Bath BA1 1HE, UK

ISBN: 1-40543-118-0

Printed in Indonesia

Produced by the Bridgewater Book Company Ltd.

NOTE

This book uses imperial, metric, and US cup measurements. Follow the same
units of measurement throughout; do not mix imperial and metric.
All spoon measurements are level: teaspoons are assumed to be 5 ml,
and tablespoons are assumed to be 15 ml. Unless otherwise stated,
milk is assumed to be whole, eggs and individual vegetables such as potatoes
are medium, and pepper is freshly ground black pepper.

The times given for each recipe are an approximate guide only
because cooking times may vary as a result of the types of oven and
other equipment used.

Recipes using raw or very lightly cooked eggs should be
avoided by infants, the elderly, pregnant women, convalescents, and anyone
suffering from an illness. Pregnant and breastfeeding women are advised to
avoid eating peanuts and peanut products.

Contents

Introduction

What constitutes a healthy diet? In one way, the answer to this question is very straightforward, while in another, it is almost impossible. It is true that a balanced intake of all the various food groups—fats, proteins, and carbohydrates—in their appropriate proportions is the ideal that

nutritionists encourage us to aim for. However, this raises a number of questions: where we are starting from, how old we are, what kind of lives we lead, whether we are men or women, and even how to estimate "a balanced intake" and "appropriate proportions"? For various reasons, many of us have let the extra weight creep on and developed eating patterns that, at best, do our bodies no favors and, at worst, make us sluggish, fat, unhappy, and ill. A low-carbohydrate diet is one very successful way of tackling these sorts of problems, revitalizing and re-energizing the system and trimming off the spare tire around the tummy.

What are carbohydrates?

The name of this food group derives from the chemical elements it contains—carbon, hydrogen, and oxygen—which form compounds such as starch and sugars. When these are eaten, the body breaks them down to release energy. They are found in a wide variety of commonly eaten foods. Grains and cereals, for example, feature in most meals, from the morning's cornflakes, through the lunchtime sandwich, to the evening plate of pasta. Potatoes are a starchy staple and dried peas, beans, and lentils are also high in carbohydrates. Many popular snacks—chocolate bars, cookies, muffins, doughnuts, and soda—are packed with sugars. Carbohydrates are comfort foods, making us feel full and satisfied.

There is a second type of carbohydrate that our bodies cannot digest and this is usually called dietary fiber. This contributes to the feeling of fullness after a meal and helps to regulate the digestive system, but the body cannot break it down to release energy. This kind of carbohydrate is found in wheat bran, fruits, dried peas, beans and lentils, nuts, and leafy green vegetables.

Energy and body weight

The body needs energy to function and it obtains this from the food consumed. Even the process of digestion uses up energy. However, the amount of energy you require depends on a number of factors. It is obvious that an Olympic athlete requires more input than a sedentary office worker, but age is also a consideration because the metabolism begins to slow down from about the age of 30. Body type, including the amount of muscle mass and lean tissue, also affects energy requirements.

Energy is measured as calories, also called kilocalories (kcal), and as kilojoules (kJ). 1 kcal equals about 4 kJ. Many of the calories consumed are used quite quickly for everyday activities, from breathing to walking up the stairs. The energy that is not used is converted by the body to be stored in the muscles or as fat. It is easy to see that if you consume more calories than you use, the body will build up a store of fat.

The following is a guide to the approximate daily calorie intake required by men and women at different life stages.

daily calorie intake

Growing children
Boys and girls—1,800–2,220 calories per day

Adults who exercise/have physical jobs
Men—2,850 calories per day
Women—2,150 calories per day

Adults who do not exercise/have sedentary jobs
Men—2,400 calories per day
Women—2,000 calories per day

Over 50s
Men—2,200 calories per day
Women—1,850 calories per day

How a low-carbohydrate diet can help

Carbohydrates are the main source of energy in our diets, with fats the second most important, so if you want to lose weight, reducing the intake of carbohydrates is a good way to do it. However, cutting them out altogether is neither sensible nor practical, because you will also be cutting out important nutrients. It is also unwise to embark on a drastic reduction of carbohydrates all at once. If you introduce this new eating pattern gradually, you will not encounter the mood swings or hunger pangs that so often go with attempts to diet and usually result in failure.

While it is true that taking in more energy than is expended is the reason why fat accumulates in the body, individual metabolism also plays a part. Some people are simply more intolerant of carbohydrates than others and can almost see their hips growing with every slice of bread. Pay attention to your body and respond to its particular requirements.

Previously, the most difficult aspect of a low-carbohydrate diet was deciding what to eat, not what to leave out. This is because much of the variety and contrast in our "normal" meals is derived from incorporating carbohydrates. Who wants a burger without a bun, steak without French fries, or meatballs without spaghetti? The problem is now solved because this book provides a wealth of recipes for delicious, low-carbohydrate dishes that are easy to make and will also satisfy the appetite. All the thinking, planning, and calorie-counting has been done for you. The recipes, based on meat, poultry, eggs, cheese, and vegetables, offer both variety and enjoyment.

For many people, a low-carbohydrate diet is a lifetime choice, used to maintain their optimum body weight. Others find it a quick way to shed a few pounds before a summer holiday or after an over-indulgent Christmas. The choice is, of course, personal, but do bear in mind that if you return to higher-carbohydrate meals, you are likely to regain the weight.

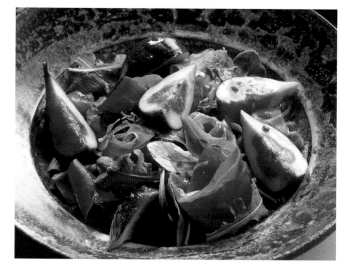

Choosing low-carbohydrate ingredients

Labels providing nutritional information on packaged foods are not always as clear and helpful as they might be. However, carbohydrate content is normally included and covers both starches and sugars. Dietary fiber, or nondigestible carbohydrates, is usually listed separately. Not all products include a measure of fiber, either because there isn't any or because figures are not available. If you take a calculator shopping with you, you may find it helpful to know that 1 gram of carbohydrate supplies about 3.75 calories or 16 kilojoules of energy.

There is no reason why you shouldn't substitute one ingredient for another in any of the recipes in this book, provided that it does not increase the carbohydrate count. While Brie contains only traces of carbohydrate, some blue cheeses may have 2 grams per 100 grams—a small difference, but it will

increase the carbohydrate count. Cauliflower contains almost twice as much carbohydrate as broccoli. Also, bear in mind that some most unexpected foods, including accompaniments and drinks, contain carbohydrates. These will contribute to the overall count. It's no good cooking a low-carbohydrate curry and serving it with a high-carbohydrate chutney. At the same time, there is no point in being obsessive. A strong mustard may contain about 19 grams of carbohydrate per ⅓ cup, but when did you last eat more than about ½ teaspoon at one sitting?

Nowadays, there are some specially manufactured low-carbohydrate products on the market, but they are often quite expensive and their labels require very close scrutiny. Jellies and spreads produced without added sugar will contain some natural fruit sugars but are generally a good buy. Low-carbohydrate baked goods may be lifesavers for the incorrigibly sweet-toothed, but they do vary in quality, while sugarfree candy and chocolates, originally produced for diabetes sufferers, have a good reputation. Other products may boast of a low-carbohydrate count per portion, but you need to check what the manufacturers regard as a portion—sometimes it's risibly small.

Soups & Appetizers

Soups are an invaluable part of a healthy low-carbohydrate eating plan, with their comforting and satisfying qualities. They also offer a wide variety of flavors and textures, as the following recipes show. Choose from a smooth vegetable soup, such as Cream of Artichoke Soup (see page 10), or a classic Bouillabaisse (see page 26) with chunks of delicious seafood. For something to really tickle the taste buds, try the Mexican-inspired Chicken, Avocado & Chipotle Soup (see page 22).

Tasty and nutritious vegetables also feature highly in the range of appetizers on offer—cool, clean-tasting cucumbers in Tsatziki (see page 37), succulent mushrooms in a Soufflé Omelet (see page 46), and sweetly smoky eggplants in the elegant Eggplant Rolls (see page 45). Or you can major on serious high-protein savories, such as Bang-Bang Chicken (see page 58).

cream of artichoke soup

serves six

1 lb 10 oz/750 g Jerusalem
    artichokes
1 lemon, thickly sliced
4 tbsp butter or margarine
2 onions, chopped
1 garlic clove, crushed
generous 1 quart vegetable stock
salt and pepper
2 bay leaves
¼ tsp ground mace or
    ground nutmeg
1 tbsp lemon juice
⅔ cup light cream or plain yogurt
TO GARNISH
coarsely grated carrot
chopped fresh parsley or cilantro

NUTRITION

Calories 190	Sugars 0g	
Protein 0.4g	Fat 2g	
Carbohydrate 0.7g	Saturates 0.7g	

1 Peel and slice the artichokes. Place in a bowl of water with the lemon slices.

2 Melt the butter in a large pan. Add the onions and garlic and cook gently for 3–4 minutes, or until soft but not colored.

3 Drain the artichokes, discarding the lemon, and add to the pan. Mix well and cook gently for 2–3 minutes without allowing to color.

4 Add the stock, salt and pepper, bay leaves, mace, and lemon juice. Bring slowly to a boil, then reduce the heat and simmer, covered, for 30 minutes, or until the vegetables are very tender.

5 Remove and discard the bay leaves. Let the soup cool slightly, then press through a strainer into a bowl. Alternatively, process the soup in a food processor or blender until smooth. If liked, a little of the soup may be only partially puréed and added to the rest of the puréed soup, to give extra texture.

6 Pour into a clean pan and bring to a boil. Adjust the seasoning if necessary and stir in the cream. Reheat gently without boiling.

7 Ladle the soup into individual serving bowls and garnish with grated carrot and chopped parsley. Serve immediately.

gazpacho

serves four

½ small cucumber

½ small green bell pepper, seeded
    and very finely chopped

1 lb 2 oz/500 g ripe tomatoes,
    peeled, or 14 oz/400 g canned
    chopped tomatoes

½ onion, coarsely chopped

2–3 garlic cloves, crushed

3 tbsp olive oil

2 tbsp white wine vinegar

1–2 tbsp lemon or lime juice

2 tbsp tomato paste

2 cups tomato juice

salt and pepper

TO SERVE

chopped green bell pepper

thinly sliced onion rings

croutons

NUTRITION

Calories 140	Sugars 12g
Protein 3g	Fat 9g
Carbohydrate 13g	Saturates 1g

1 Coarsely grate the cucumber into a large bowl and add the chopped bell pepper.

2 Place the tomatoes, onion, and garlic in a food processor or blender. Add the oil, vinegar, lemon juice, and tomato paste and process until smooth. Alternatively, finely chop the tomatoes and finely grate the onion, then mix together. Add the garlic, oil, vinegar, lemon juice, and tomato paste and mix well.

3 Add the tomato mixture to the bowl and mix well, then add the tomato juice and mix again.

4 Season to taste with salt and pepper. Cover and let chill in the refrigerator for 6 hours, or preferably longer, to let the flavors meld together.

5 Prepare the side dishes of chopped bell pepper, thinly sliced onion rings, and croutons and arrange them in serving bowls. Ladle the soup into cold bowls, handing round the side dishes separately.

chicken consommé

serves eight–ten

1½ quarts chicken stock

⅔ cup medium sherry

4 egg whites, plus eggshells

salt and pepper

4 oz/115 g cooked chicken,
thinly sliced

COOK'S TIP

Consommé is usually garnished with freshly cooked pasta shapes, noodles, rice, or lightly cooked vegetables. For a low-carbohydrate option, you could garnish it with omelet strips, drained first on paper towels.

NUTRITION

Calories 96	Sugars 1g
Protein 11g	Fat 1g
Carbohydrate 1g	Saturates 0.4g

1 Place the stock and sherry in a large heavy-bottom pan and heat gently for 5 minutes.

2 Add the egg whites and the eggshells to the stock and whisk until the mixture begins to boil.

3 Remove the pan from the heat and let the mixture subside for 10 minutes. Repeat this heating and subsiding process 3 times. This enables the egg white to trap the sediments in the stock to clarify the soup. Let the consommé cool for 5 minutes.

4 Carefully place a piece of fine cheesecloth over a clean pan. Ladle the soup over the cheesecloth and strain into the pan.

5 Repeat this process twice, then gently reheat the consommé.

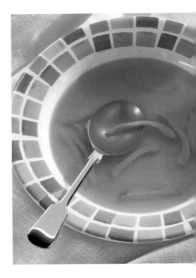

Season to taste with salt and pepper, then add the cooked chicken slices. Pour the soup into a warmed serving dish or individual serving bowls.

6 Garnish with any of the suggestions in the Cook's Tip and serve.

crab & ginger soup

serves four

1 carrot, chopped

1 leek, chopped

1 bay leaf

3½ cups fish stock

2 medium-size cooked crabs

1-inch/2.5-cm piece fresh
  gingerroot, grated

1 tsp light soy sauce

½ tsp ground star anise

salt and pepper

NUTRITION

Calories 145	Sugars 2.4g
Protein 40g	Fat 5.7g
Carbohydrate 2.7g	Saturates 2.6g

1 Place the carrot, leek, bay leaf, and stock in a large pan and bring to a boil over medium heat. Reduce the heat, then cover and let simmer for 10 minutes, or until the vegetables are nearly tender.

2 Meanwhile, remove the meat from the cooked crabs. Break off the claws and break the joints, then remove the meat (you may need a fork or skewer for this). Add the crabmeat to the stock in the pan.

3 Add the ginger, soy sauce, and star anise to the stock and bring to a boil. Reduce the heat and let simmer for 10 minutes, or until the vegetables are tender and the crab is heated through. Season to taste with salt and pepper.

4 Ladle the soup into 4 warmed serving bowls and garnish with crab claws. Serve immediately.

COOK'S TIP

To prepare cooked crab, loosen the meat from the shell by banging the back of the underside with a clenched fist. Stand the crab on its edge with the shell toward you. Force the shell from the body with your thumbs. Twist off the legs and claws and remove the meat. Twist off the tail and discard. Remove and discard the gills from each side of the body. Cut the body in half along the center and remove the meat. Scoop the brown meat from the shell.

COOK'S TIP

If fresh crabmeat is unavailable, use drained canned crabmeat or thawed frozen crabmeat instead.

fish soup with won tons

serves four

4½ oz/125 g cooked,
  shelled shrimp
1 tsp snipped fresh chives, plus
  extra to garnish
1 small garlic clove, finely chopped
1 tbsp vegetable oil
12 won ton skins
1 small egg, beaten
3½ cups fish stock
6 oz/175 g white fish fillet, diced
dash of chili sauce
1 fresh red chili, sliced, to garnish

NUTRITION

Calories 115	Sugars 0g
Protein 16g	Fat 5g
Carbohydrate 1g	Saturates 1g

VARIATION

You can replace the shrimp with cooked crabmeat for an alternative flavor.

1 Coarsely chop a fourth of the shrimp and mix together with the chives and garlic.

2 Heat the oil in a preheated wok or large heavy-bottom skillet until it is really hot.

3 Stir-fry the shrimp mixture for 1–2 minutes. Remove from the heat and let cool completely.

4 Spread out the won ton skins on a counter. Spoon a little of the shrimp filling into the center of each skin. Brush the edges of the skins with beaten egg and press the edges together, scrunching them to form a "moneybag" shape. Reserve while you are preparing the soup.

5 Pour the stock into a large pan and bring to a boil. Add the fish and the remaining shrimp and cook for 5 minutes.

6 Add chili sauce to taste, then add the won tons and cook for an additional 5 minutes.

7 Spoon into warmed bowls and garnish with the sliced chili and extra snipped chives, then serve.

hot & sour soup

serves four

12 oz/350 g whole raw or cooked
   shrimp in shells

1 tbsp vegetable oil

1 lemongrass stem,
   coarsely chopped

2 fresh kaffir lime leaves, shredded

1 fresh green chili, seeded
   and chopped

1 quart chicken or fish stock

1 lime

1 tbsp Thai fish sauce

salt and pepper

1 fresh red Thai chili, seeded and
   thinly sliced

1 scallion, thinly sliced

1 tbsp finely chopped cilantro,
   to garnish

NUTRITION

Calories 71	Sugars 0g
Protein 8g	Fat 4g
Carbohydrate 1g	Saturates 0g

1 Shell the shrimp and reserve the shells. Cut a slit along the back of each shrimp and remove the black vein. Place in a bowl, cover, and chill.

2 Heat the oil in a large heavy-bottom pan. Add the shrimp shells and stir-fry for 3–4 minutes, or until they turn pink. Add the lemongrass, lime leaves, green chili, and stock. Pare a thin strip of rind from the lime and grate the rest. Add the grated rind to the pan.

3 Bring to a boil, then reduce the heat, and let simmer, covered, for 20 minutes.

4 Strain the liquid and pour it back into the pan. Squeeze the juice from the lime and add to the pan with the fish sauce and salt and pepper to taste.

5 Bring to a boil, then reduce the heat and add the shrimp. Simmer for 2–3 minutes.

6 Add the red chili and scallion. Sprinkle with the chopped cilantro and lime rind strip and serve.

spinach & tofu soup

serves four

8 oz/225 g firm tofu
(drained weight)
4½ oz/125 g fresh spinach leaves
3 cups water or
vegetable stock
1 tbsp light soy sauce
salt and pepper

COOK'S TIP

Soup is an integral part of a
Chinese meal; it is usually
presented in a large bowl placed
in the center of the table, and
consumed as the meal
progresses. It serves as a
refresher between different
dishes and as a beverage
throughout the meal.

NUTRITION

Calories 33	Sugar 1g
Protein 4g	Fat 2g
Carbohydrate 1g	Saturates 0.2g

1 Using a sharp knife to avoid squashing it, cut the tofu into small cubes about ¼ inch/5 mm thick.

2 Rinse the spinach leaves thoroughly under cold running water and drain well.

3 Cut the spinach leaves into small pieces or shreds, discarding any discolored leaves and tough stems. (If possible, use fresh young spinach leaves, which have not yet developed tough ribs. Otherwise, it is important to cut out all the ribs and stems for this soup.) Reserve the spinach until required.

4 Bring the water to a rolling boil in a preheated wok or large heavy-bottom skillet.

5 Add the tofu and soy sauce, then return to a boil and simmer for 2 minutes over medium heat.

6 Add the spinach and simmer for an additional 1 minute, stirring gently. Skim the surface of the soup to make it clear and season to taste with salt and pepper.

7 Transfer the soup to a warmed soup tureen or warmed individual serving bowls and serve with chopsticks and a broad, shallow spoon.

chicken soup with almonds

serves four

1 large or 2 small skinless, boneless
    chicken breasts
1 tbsp corn oil
4 scallions, thinly sliced
    diagonally
1 carrot, cut into julienne strips
3 cups chicken stock
finely grated rind of ½ lemon
½ cup ground almonds
1 tbsp light soy sauce
1 tbsp lemon juice
salt and pepper
¼ cup slivered almonds,
    toasted

NUTRITION

Calories 219	Sugars 2g
Protein 18g	Fat 15g
Carbohydrate 2g	Saturates 2g

1 Cut each chicken breast into 4 strips lengthwise, then slice very thinly across the grain to give shreds of meat.

2 Heat the oil in a preheated wok, swirling it around until really hot.

3 Add the scallions and cook for 2 minutes, then add the chicken and toss it for 3–4 minutes, or until sealed and almost cooked through, stirring constantly. Add the carrot strips and stir well.

4 Add the stock to the wok and bring to a boil. Add the lemon rind, ground almonds, soy sauce, lemon juice, and plenty of salt and pepper. Return to a boil and let simmer, uncovered, for 5 minutes, stirring occasionally.

5 Adjust the seasoning if necessary, then add most of the toasted almonds and continue to cook for an additional 1–2 minutes.

6 Serve the soup hot, in individual serving bowls, sprinkled with the remaining toasted almonds.

COOK'S TIP
To toast slivered almonds, place them in a dry skillet over medium heat and stir until lightly browned. Keep a close eye on them because they burn very easily.

chicken, avocado & chipotle soup

serves four

1¼ quarts chicken stock

2–3 garlic cloves, finely chopped

1–2 dried chipotle chilies, cut into
very thin strips (see Cook's Tip)

1 avocado

lime or lemon juice, for tossing

3–5 scallions, thinly sliced

12–14 oz/350–400 g cooked
chicken breast meat, torn or cut
into shreds or thin strips

2 tbsp chopped cilantro

1 lime, cut into wedges,
to serve

NUTRITION

Calories 216	Sugars 1g
Protein 28g	Fat 11g
Carbohydrate 2g	Saturates 2g

VARIATION

Add 14 oz/400 g canned, drained
chickpeas to the bowls with the
scallions, chicken, avocado,
and cilantro.

1 Place the stock in a large heavy-bottom pan with the garlic and chilies and bring to a boil.

2 Meanwhile, cut the avocado in half around the pit. Twist apart, then remove the pit with a knife. Carefully peel off the skin and dice the flesh, then toss in lime juice to prevent discoloration.

3 Arrange the scallions, chicken, avocado, and cilantro in the bottom of 4 soup bowls or in a large serving bowl.

4 Ladle hot stock over and serve with lime wedges.

COOK'S TIP

Chipotle chilies are smoked and dried jalapeño chilies. They are available canned or dried from specialty stores. They add a distinctive smoky flavor to dishes and are very hot. Use chipotles canned in adobo marinade for this recipe, if possible. Drain the canned version before using. Dried chipotles need to be reconstituted before using by soaking in hot water until soft.

chili & watercress soup

serves four

1 tbsp corn oil

9 oz/250 g smoked tofu (drained weight), sliced

3 oz/85 g shiitake mushrooms, sliced

2 tbsp chopped cilantro

4½ oz/125 g watercress

1 fresh red chili, seeded and finely sliced, to garnish

STOCK

1 tbsp tamarind pulp

2 dried red chilies, chopped

2 fresh kaffir lime leaves, torn in half

1-inch/2.5-cm piece fresh gingerroot, chopped

2-inch/5-cm piece fresh galangal, chopped

1 lemongrass stem, chopped

1 onion, cut into fourths

4 cups cold water

1 Place all the ingredients for the stock in a pan and bring to a boil.

2 Simmer the stock for 5 minutes. Remove the pan from the heat and strain, reserving the stock.

3 Heat the oil in a preheated wok or large heavy-bottomed skillet. Add the tofu and cook over high heat for 2 minutes, stirring constantly so that the tofu cooks evenly on both sides. Add the strained stock to the skillet.

4 Add the mushrooms and cilantro and boil for 3 minutes.

5 Add the watercress and boil for an additional 1 minute. Serve, garnished with red chili slices.

NUTRITION	
Calories 90	Sugars 1g
Protein 7g	Fat 6g
Carbohydrate 2g	Saturates 1g

VARIATION

You might like to try a mixture of different types of mushroom. Oyster, white, and straw mushrooms are all suitable.

spinach & ginger soup

serves four

2 tbsp corn oil

1 onion, chopped

2 garlic cloves, finely chopped

1-inch piece/2.5-cm piece fresh
   gingerroot, finely chopped

9 oz/250 g fresh young
   spinach leaves

1 small lemongrass stem,
   finely chopped

4 cups chicken or
   vegetable stock

1 small potato, chopped

1 tbsp rice wine or dry sherry

salt and pepper

1 tsp sesame oil

NUTRITION

Calories 38	Sugars 0.8g
Protein 3.2g	Fat 1.8g
Carbohydrate 2.4g	Saturates 0.2g

1 Heat the corn oil in a large pan. Add the onion, garlic, and ginger and stir-fry gently for 3–4 minutes, or until softened but not browned.

2 Reserve 2–3 small spinach leaves. Add the remaining leaves and lemongrass to the pan, stirring until the spinach is wilted. Add the stock and potato to the pan and bring to a boil. Reduce the heat, then cover and simmer for 10 minutes.

3 Transfer the soup to a food processor or blender and process until completely smooth.

4 Return the soup to the pan and add the rice wine, then season to taste with salt and pepper. Heat until just about to boil.

VARIATION

To make a creamy-textured spinach and coconut soup, stir in 4 tablespoons creamed coconut, or replace 1¼ cups of the stock with coconut milk. Serve the soup with fresh coconut shavings sprinkled on the top.

5 Finely shred the reserved spinach leaves and sprinkle some over the top. Drizzle with a few drops of sesame oil and serve hot, garnished with the remaining finely shredded spinach leaves.

bouillabaisse

serves six–eight

1 lb/450 g raw jumbo shrimp

1 lb 10 oz/750 g firm white fish
fillets, such as sea bass, snapper,
or angler fish

4 tbsp olive oil

grated rind of 1 orange

1 large garlic clove, finely chopped

½ tsp chili paste or harissa

1 fennel bulb, finely chopped

1 large onion, finely chopped

8 oz/225 g potatoes, halved and
thinly sliced

9 oz/250 g raw scallops, shelled

salt and pepper

STOCK

1 large leek, sliced

1 onion, halved and sliced

1 red bell pepper, seeded and sliced

3–4 tomatoes, cored and cut
into 8 wedges

4 garlic cloves, sliced

1 bay leaf

pinch of saffron threads

½ tsp fennel seeds

2½ cups water

1 quart fish stock

1 Shell the shrimp and reserve the shells. Cut the fish fillets into pieces about 2 inches/5 cm square. Trim off any ragged edges and reserve. Place the fish in a bowl with 2 tablespoons of the oil, the orange rind, chopped garlic, and chili paste. Turn to coat well, then cover and chill the shrimp and fish separately in the refrigerator.

2 For the stock, heat 1 tablespoon of the remaining oil in a large pan over medium heat. Add the leek, sliced onion, and bell pepper. Cover and cook for 5 minutes, stirring, until the onion softens. Stir in the tomatoes, sliced garlic, bay leaf, saffron, fennel seeds, shrimp shells, fish trimmings, water, and stock. Bring to a boil, then reduce the heat and simmer, covered, for 30 minutes. Strain the stock.

3 Heat the remaining oil in a separate large pan. Add the fennel and chopped onion and cook for 5 minutes, or until softened. Add the stock and potatoes and bring to a boil. Reduce the heat and cover, then cook for 12–15 minutes, or until tender.

4 Reduce the heat and add the fish, thick pieces first and thinner ones after 2–3 minutes. Add the shrimp and scallops and let simmer until all the seafood is cooked and opaque throughout.

5 Taste and adjust the seasoning if necessary. Ladle into warmed bowls and serve.

NUTRITION	
Calories 273	Sugars 4g
Protein 36g	Fat 9g
Carbohydrate 13g	Saturates 2g

celery root, leek & potato soup

serves four–six

1 tbsp butter

1 onion, chopped

2 large leeks, halved lengthwise
    and sliced

1 celery root (about 1 lb 10 oz/
    750 g), peeled and diced

1 potato, diced

1 carrot, cut into fourths and
    thinly sliced

1 quart water

⅛ tsp dried marjoram

1 bay leaf

salt and pepper

freshly grated nutmeg

celery leaves, to garnish

NUTRITION

Calories 81	Sugars 5g
Protein 3g	Fat 3g
Carbohydrate 11g	Saturates 2g

1 Melt the butter in a large pan over medium heat. Add the onion and leeks and cook for 4 minutes, stirring frequently, until just softened but not colored.

2 Add the celery root, potato, carrot, water, marjoram, bay leaf, and a large pinch of salt. Bring to a boil, then reduce the heat and let simmer, covered, for 25 minutes, or until the vegetables are tender. Remove and discard the bay leaf.

3 Let the soup cool slightly. Transfer to a food processor or blender and process until smooth. (If using a food processor, strain off the cooking liquid and reserve. Process the soup solids, moistened with a little cooking liquid, then combine with the remaining liquid.)

4 Return the soup to a clean pan and stir to blend. Season to taste with salt, pepper, and nutmeg. Stir constantly until reheated.

5 Ladle the soup into warmed soup bowls and garnish with celery leaves, then serve.

leek, potato & bacon soup

serves four–six

2 tbsp butter

1 cup diced potatoes

4 leeks, shredded

2 garlic cloves, crushed

⅓ cup diced smoked bacon

3½ cups vegetable stock

1 cup heavy cream

2 tbsp chopped fresh parsley

salt and pepper

TO GARNISH

vegetable oil

1 leek, shredded

NUTRITION

Calories 316		Sugars 3g	
Protein 11g		Fat 27g	
Carbohydrate 9g		Saturates 15g	

1 Melt the butter in a large pan. Add the potatoes, leeks, garlic, and bacon and cook gently for 5 minutes, stirring constantly.

2 Add the stock and bring to a boil. Reduce the heat, then cover and let simmer for 20 minutes, or until the potatoes are cooked. Stir in the cream and mix well.

3 Meanwhile, make the garnish. Half fill a pan with oil and heat to 350–375°F/180–190°C, or until a cube of bread browns in 30 seconds. Add the shredded leek and deep-fry for 1 minute, or until browned and crisp, taking care because it contains water. Drain the shredded leek thoroughly on paper towels and reserve.

4 Reserve a few pieces of potato, leek, and bacon. Transfer the rest of the soup, in batches, to a food processor or blender and process each batch for 30 seconds. Return the soup to a clean pan and heat through.

5 Stir in the reserved vegetables, bacon, and chopped parsley, then season to taste with salt and pepper. Pour into warmed soup bowls and garnish with the fried leeks.

VARIATION

For a lighter soup, omit the cream and stir plain yogurt into the soup at the end of the cooking time.

exotic mushroom soup

serves four

1 oz/25 g dried porcini mushrooms

1½ cups boiling water

4½ oz/125 g fresh porcini or other
exotic mushrooms

2 tsp olive oil

1 celery stalk, chopped

1 carrot, chopped

1 onion, chopped

3 garlic cloves, crushed

1 quart vegetable stock
or water

leaves from 2 fresh thyme sprigs

salt and pepper

1 tbsp butter

3 tbsp dry or medium sherry

2–3 tbsp sour cream

chopped fresh parsley, to garnish

NUTRITION

Calories 130	Sugars 5g
Protein 3g	Fat 9g
Carbohydrate 6g	Saturates 5g

1 Place the dried mushrooms in a heatproof bowl and pour the boiling water over them. Let soak for 10–15 minutes.

2 Brush or wipe the fresh mushrooms. Trim and reserve the stems. Slice any large mushroom caps.

3 Heat the oil in a large pan. Add the celery, carrot, onion, and mushroom stems and cook, stirring frequently, for 8 minutes, or until the onion begins to color. Stir in the garlic and cook for an additional 1 minute.

4 Add the stock, thyme leaves, and a pinch of salt. Using a slotted spoon, transfer the soaked dried mushrooms to the pan. Strain the soaking liquid through a cheesecloth-lined strainer into the pan. Bring to a boil, then reduce the heat and simmer gently, partially covered, for 30–40 minutes, or until the carrots are tender.

5 Remove the pan from the heat and let cool slightly, then transfer the soup solids with enough of the cooking liquid to moisten to a food processor or blender and process until smooth. Return the soup to the pan and combine with the remaining cooking liquid, then cover and simmer gently.

6 Meanwhile, melt the butter in a skillet. Add the fresh mushroom caps and season to taste with salt and pepper. Cook, stirring occasionally, for 8 minutes, or until the mushrooms begin to color, stirring more frequently as the liquid evaporates. When the skillet becomes dry, add the sherry and cook briefly.

7 Add the mushrooms and sherry to the soup. Taste and adjust the seasoning, if necessary. Ladle into warmed soup bowls, place a spoonful of sour cream in each, and garnish with parsley. Serve immediately.

chicken & corn soup

serves four

2 tsp corn oil

1 tbsp butter or margarine

1 small onion, finely chopped

1 chicken leg quarter or
  2–3 drumsticks

1 tbsp all-purpose flour

2½ cups chicken stock

½ small red, yellow, or orange bell
  pepper, seeded and
  finely chopped

2 large tomatoes, peeled
  and chopped

2 tsp tomato paste

scant 1¼ cups corn kernels, drained

generous pinch of dried oregano

¼ tsp ground coriander

salt and pepper

chopped fresh parsley, to garnish

NUTRITION

Calories 200	Sugars 6g
Protein 10g	Fat 12g
Carbohydrate 13g	Saturates 5g

1 Heat the oil and butter in a pan. Add the onion and cook until beginning to soften. Cut the chicken quarter, if using, into 2 pieces. Add the chicken and cook until golden brown.

2 Add the flour and cook for 1–2 minutes. Add the stock and bring to a boil, then reduce the heat and simmer for 5 minutes.

3 Add the bell pepper, tomatoes, tomato paste, corn, oregano, coriander, and salt and pepper to taste. Cover and let simmer gently for 20 minutes, or until the chicken is very tender.

4 Remove the chicken from the soup, then strip off the flesh and chop finely. Return the chopped meat to the soup.

5 Taste and adjust the seasoning if necessary and simmer for an additional 2–3 minutes. Sprinkle with parsley and serve very hot.

provençal fish soup

serves four–six

1 tbsp olive oil

2 onions, finely chopped

1 small leek, thinly sliced

1 small carrot, finely chopped

1 celery stalk, finely chopped

1 small fennel bulb, finely
  chopped (optional)

3 garlic cloves, finely chopped

1 cup dry white wine

14 oz/400 g canned tomatoes

1 bay leaf

pinch of fennel seeds

2 strips of orange rind

¼ tsp saffron threads

1 quart water

12 oz/350 g white fish
  fillets, skinned

salt and pepper

celery leaves, to garnish (optional)

NUTRITION

Calories 122	Sugars 6g
Protein 12g	Fat 3g
Carbohydrate 7g	Saturates 0g

1 Heat the oil in a large pan. Add the onions and cook, stirring occasionally, for 5 minutes, or until softened. Add the leek, carrot, celery, fennel, if using, and garlic and cook for an additional 4–5 minutes, or until the leek is wilted.

2 Add the wine and simmer for 1 minute. Add the tomatoes, bay leaf, fennel seeds, orange rind, saffron, and water. Bring just to a boil. Reduce the heat and simmer gently, covered, stirring occasionally, for 30 minutes.

3 Add the fish and cook for an additional 20–30 minutes, or until it flakes easily. Remove and discard the bay leaf and orange rind.

4 Remove the pan from the heat and let cool slightly, then transfer to a food processor or blender and process to a smooth purée, working in batches if necessary. (If using a food processor, strain the cooking liquid and reserve. Process the soup solids with enough cooking liquid to moisten them, then combine with the remaining liquid.)

5 Return the soup to the pan. Season to taste with salt and pepper, if necessary, then simmer for 5–10 minutes, or until heated through. Ladle into warmed bowls and garnish with celery leaves, if desired. Serve.

beef broth

serves four

7 oz/200 g celery root, finely diced

2 large carrots, finely diced

2 tsp chopped fresh marjoram

2 tsp chopped fresh parsley

2 plum tomatoes, peeled, seeded, and diced

salt and pepper

BEEF STOCK

1 lb 4 oz/550 g beef stewing steak, cut into large cubes

1 lb 10 oz/750 g veal, beef, or pork bones

2 onions, cut into fourths

2¼ quarts water

4 garlic cloves, sliced

2 carrots, sliced

1 large leek, sliced

1 celery stalk, cut into 2-inch/ 5-cm pieces

1 bay leaf

4–5 fresh thyme sprigs or ¼ tsp dried thyme

salt

NUTRITION

Calories 21	Sugars 3g
Protein 1g	Fat 1g
Carbohydrate 4g	Saturates 0g

1 Preheat the oven to 375°F/190°C. To make the stock, trim the fat from the beef and place the beef and fat in a large roasting pan with the bones and onions. Roast in the oven for 30–40 minutes, or until browned, turning once or twice. Transfer to a large flameproof casserole and drain off the beef fat.

2 Add the water (it should cover by at least 2 inches/5 cm) and bring to a boil. Skim off any foam, then reduce the heat and add the garlic, carrots, leek, celery, bay leaf, thyme, and a pinch of salt. Simmer for 4 hours, skimming occasionally. If the ingredients emerge from the liquid, top up with water. Strain the stock through a cheesecloth-lined strainer into a container and remove as much fat as possible. Use the meat in another recipe and discard the bones and vegetables.

3 Gently boil the stock until reduced to 1¼ quarts. Taste and adjust the seasoning if necessary.

4 Bring a pan of salted water to the boil. Add the celery root and carrots, then reduce the heat and simmer, covered, for 15 minutes, or until tender. Drain. Add the herbs to the beef stock. Divide the vegetables and tomatoes between warmed soup bowls and ladle over the stock. Serve.

aïoli

serves four

4 large garlic cloves, or to taste
  (see Cook's Tip)
sea salt and pepper
2 large egg yolks
1¼ cups extra virgin olive oil
1–2 tbsp lemon juice
1 tbsp fresh white bread crumbs
TO SERVE
selection of raw vegetables, such as
  sliced red bell peppers, zucchini
  slices, whole scallions, and
  tomato wedges
selection of blanched and cooled
  vegetables, such as baby
  artichoke hearts, cauliflower or
  broccoli florets, or green beans

COOK'S TIP

The amount of garlic in a traditional Provençal aïoli is a matter of personal taste. Local cooks use 2 cloves per person as a rule of thumb, but this version is slightly milder, although still bursting with flavor.

NUTRITION	
Calories 239	Sugars 0g
Protein 1g	Fat 26g
Carbohydrate 1g	Saturates 4g

1 Finely chop the garlic on a cutting board. Add a pinch of sea salt to the garlic and use the tip and broad side of a knife to work the garlic and salt into a smooth paste.

2 Transfer the garlic paste to a food processor or blender. Add the egg yolks and process until well blended, scraping down the side of the bowl with a rubber spatula, if necessary.

3 With the motor running, slowly pour in the oil in a steady stream through the feeder tube, processing until a thick mayonnaise forms.

4 Add 1 tablespoon of the lemon juice and all the bread crumbs and process again. Taste and add more lemon juice if necessary. Season to taste with sea salt and pepper.

5 Place the aïoli in a bowl, then cover, and let chill until ready to serve. To serve, place the bowl of aïoli on a large platter and surround with a selection of raw and lightly blanched vegetables.

tsatziki

serves twelve

2 large cucumbers

2½ cups thick plain yogurt

3 garlic cloves, crushed

1 tbsp finely chopped fresh dill

1 tbsp extra virgin olive oil

salt and pepper

TO GARNISH

1 tbsp sesame seeds

cayenne pepper

fresh dill sprigs (optional)

NUTRITION

Calories 75		Sugars 2g	
Protein 4g		Fat 6g	
Carbohydrate 2g		Saturates 3g	

1 Using the coarse side of a grater, grate the cucumbers into a bowl lined with an absorbent, perforated kitchen cloth. Pull up the corners of the cloth to make a tight bundle and squeeze very hard to extract all the moisture (see Cook's Tip).

2 Place the cucumber in a bowl and stir in the yogurt, garlic, dill, and oil. Season to taste with salt and pepper. Cover with plastic wrap and let chill for at least 3 hours so that the flavors blend.

3 When ready to serve, remove the dip from the refrigerator and stir. Taste and adjust the seasoning if necessary.

4 Place the sesame seeds in a small, ungreased skillet and dry-fry them over medium heat until they turn golden and begin to give off their aroma. Immediately pour them out of the skillet onto the tsatziki—they will sizzle.

5 Sprinkle some cayenne onto a plate. Lightly dip the tip of a dry pastry brush into the cayenne, then tap a light sprinkling of cayenne over the tsatziki. Garnish with dill sprigs, if using. Ungarnished tsatziki will keep for up to 3 days in the refrigerator.

COOK'S TIP

It is essential to squeeze all the moisture out of the cucumbers in Step 1, or the dip will be unpleasantly watery and will separate.

authentic guacamole

serves four

1 ripe tomato

2 limes

2–3 ripe small–medium avocados
or 1–2 large ones

¼–½ onion, finely chopped

pinch of ground cumin

pinch of mild chili powder

½–1 fresh green chili, such as
jalapeño or serrano, seeded and
finely chopped

1 tbsp finely chopped cilantro
leaves, plus extra to garnish

salt (optional)

vegetable sticks, to serve
(optional)

NUTRITION

Calories 212	Sugars 1g
Protein 2g	Fat 21g
Carbohydrate 3g	Saturates 4g

1 Place the tomato in a heatproof bowl, then cover with boiling water and let stand for 30 seconds. Drain and plunge into cold water. Peel off the skin. Cut the tomato in half, then seed and chop the flesh.

2 Squeeze the juice from the limes into a small bowl. Cut 1 avocado in half around the pit. Twist the 2 halves apart in opposite directions, then remove the pit with a knife. Peel off the skin, then dice the flesh and toss in the lime juice to prevent the flesh discoloring. Repeat with the remaining avocados. Mash the avocado flesh coarsely with a fork.

3 Add the onion, tomato, cumin, chili powder, fresh chili, and cilantro to the avocados. If using as a dip for tortilla chips, do not add salt. If using as a dip for vegetable sticks, add salt to taste.

4 To serve the guacamole, transfer to a serving dish and garnish with cilantro, then serve with vegetable sticks.

VARIATION

Try spooning guacamole into soups, especially chicken or seafood. Spoon guacamole over refried beans and melted cheese, then eat it with a salsa of your choice.

hummus

serves eight

1 cup dried chickpeas

2 large garlic cloves

scant ½ cup extra virgin olive oil,
plus extra for drizzling

2½ tbsp tahini

1 tbsp lemon juice

salt and pepper

paprika

cilantro sprigs, to garnish

vegetable crudités, to serve

NUTRITION

Calories 204	Sugars 1g
Protein 7g	Fat 14g
Carbohydrate 13g	Saturates 2g

1 Place the chickpeas in a bowl. Pour in at least twice their volume of water and soak for 12 hours, or until they double in size.

2 Drain the chickpeas. Place them in a large flameproof casserole or pan and add twice their volume of water. Bring to a boil and boil vigorously for 10 minutes, skimming the surface.

3 Reduce the heat and let simmer, skimming the surface occasionally, for 1–2 hours, or until the chickpeas are tender.

4 Meanwhile, cut the garlic in half, then remove and discard the green or white cores and coarsely chop the cloves. Reserve.

5 Drain the chickpeas, reserving 4 tablespoons of the cooking liquid. Place the oil, garlic, tahini, and lemon juice in a food processor and process to a smooth paste.

6 Add the chickpeas and pulse until they are finely ground but the hummus is still lightly textured. Add a little of the reserved cooking liquid if the mixture is too thick. Season to taste with salt and pepper.

7 Scrape the hummus into a bowl, then cover and chill in the refrigerator until ready to serve. Drizzle with some oil and sprinkle a little paprika over. Garnish with cilantro and serve with vegetable crudités.

parsley, chicken & ham pâté

serves four

8 oz/225 g skinless, boneless lean
    chicken, cooked

3½ oz/100 g lean cooked ham

small bunch of fresh parsley

1 tsp grated lime rind, plus extra
    to garnish

2 tbsp lime juice

1 garlic clove, peeled

½ cup lowfat cream cheese

salt and pepper

TO SERVE

lime wedges

crispbread

NUTRITION

Calories 119	Sugars 2g
Protein 20g	Fat 3g
Carbohydrate 2g	Saturates 1g

1 Coarsely dice the chicken. Trim off and discard any fat from the ham and dice the meat. Place the chicken and ham in a food processor.

2 Add the parsley, lime rind and juice, and garlic and process until finely ground. Alternatively, finely chop the chicken, ham, parsley, and garlic and place in a bowl. Gently stir in the lime rind and juice.

COOK'S TIP

Most types of crispbreads contain around ⅛ oz/6 g of carbohydrate per slice.

3 Transfer the mixture to a bowl and stir in the cream cheese. Season to taste with salt and pepper, then cover with plastic wrap and chill in the refrigerator for 30 minutes.

4 Spoon the pâté into individual serving dishes and garnish with extra grated lime rind. Serve the pâté with lime wedges and crispbread.

41

fat horses

serves four

2 tbsp creamed coconut

4 oz/115 g lean pork

4 oz/115 g skinless, boneless
   chicken breast

4 oz/115 g canned crabmeat,
   drained

2 eggs

2 garlic cloves, crushed

4 scallions, chopped

1 tbsp Thai fish sauce

1 tbsp chopped cilantro leaves
   and stems

1 tbsp raw brown sugar

salt and pepper

butter, for greasing

TO GARNISH

finely sliced daikon or turnip

fresh chive lengths

fresh chili flowers (see page 154)

cilantro sprigs

NUTRITION

Calories 195	Sugars 1g
Protein 23g	Fat 11g
Carbohydrate 1g	Saturates 6g

1 Mix the coconut with 3 tablespoons of hot water. Stir to dissolve the coconut.

2 Place the pork, chicken, and crabmeat in a food processor and process briefly for 10–15 seconds, or until ground. Alternatively, chop them finely by hand and place in a large bowl.

3 Add the coconut mixture to the food processor with the eggs, garlic, scallions, fish sauce, cilantro, and sugar. Season to taste with salt and pepper and process for an additional few seconds. Alternatively, mix these ingredients into the chopped pork, chicken, and crabmeat.

4 Grease 6 ramekin dishes with a little butter. Spoon in the ground mixture, smoothing the surface. Place them in a steamer, then set the steamer over a pan of gently simmering water. Cook for 30 minutes, or until set.

5 Lift out the dishes and let cool for a few minutes. Run a knife around the edge of each dish, then invert onto warmed plates. Serve immediately, garnished with finely sliced daikon, chive lengths, a red chili flower, and cilantro sprigs.

eggplant dip

serves six–eight

2 large eggplants

1 tomato

1 garlic clove, chopped

4 tbsp extra virgin olive oil

2 tbsp lemon juice

2 tbsp pine nuts, lightly toasted

salt and pepper

2 scallions, finely chopped

fresh vegetables, to serve

TO GARNISH

ground cumin

2 tbsp finely chopped fresh
    flatleaf parsley

NUTRITION	
Calories 90	Sugars 2g
Protein 1g	Fat 8g
Carbohydrate 2g	Saturates 1g

1 Preheat the oven to 450°F/230°C. Using a fork or metal skewer, pierce the eggplants all over. Place them on a large cookie sheet and roast in the preheated oven for 20–25 minutes, or until they are very soft.

2 Use a folded dish towel to remove the eggplants from the cookie sheet and let cool.

3 Place the tomato in a heatproof bowl and pour boiling water over to cover. Let stand for 30 seconds. Drain, then plunge into cold water to prevent it cooking. Peel the tomato, then cut in half and scoop out the seeds with a teaspoon. Finely dice the flesh and reserve.

4 Cut the cooled eggplants in half lengthwise. Scoop out the flesh with a spoon and transfer to a food processor. Add the garlic, oil, lemon juice, and pine nuts and season to taste with salt and pepper. Process until smooth. Alternatively, mash by hand.

5 Scrape the mixture into a bowl and stir in the scallions and diced tomato. Cover and let chill for 30 minutes before serving.

6 Garnish the spread with a pinch of cumin and chopped parsley, then serve with fresh vegetables.

eggplant rolls

serves four

2 eggplants, thinly sliced
    lengthwise

salt and pepper

5 tbsp olive oil, plus extra
    for oiling

1 garlic clove, crushed

4 tbsp pesto

6 oz/175 g mozzarella cheese,
    grated

fresh basil leaves, torn into pieces,
    plus extra leaves to garnish

NUTRITION

Calories 278	Sugars 2g
Protein 4g	Fat 28g
Carbohydrate 2g	Saturates 7g

COOK'S TIP

Most eggplants produced commercially these days do not have bitter juices that must be removed before cooking. Nevertheless, salting is a good idea if the eggplants are to be fried, because it prevents them absorbing too much oil.

1 Preheat the oven to 350°F/180°C. Sprinkle the eggplant slices liberally with salt and let stand for 10–15 minutes. Turn the slices over and repeat. Rinse well with cold water and drain on paper towels.

2 Heat the oil in a large skillet. Add the garlic and eggplant slices, a few at a time, and fry the eggplant lightly on both sides. Remove with a slotted spoon and drain on paper towels.

3 Spread a little pesto onto one side of each of the eggplant slices. Top with the grated mozzarella cheese and sprinkle with the torn basil leaves. Season with a little salt and pepper. Roll up the slices and secure them with wooden toothpicks.

4 Arrange the eggplant rolls in an oiled ovenproof baking dish and bake in the preheated oven for 8–10 minutes.

5 Transfer the eggplant rolls to a warmed serving plate. Sprinkle with basil leaves and serve.

soufflé omelet

serves four

6 oz/175 g cherry tomatoes

8 oz/225 g mixed mushrooms, such
   as white, cremini or portabello,
   shiitake, and oyster

4 tbsp vegetable stock

small bunch of fresh thyme, tied
   with string

4 eggs, separated

½ cup water

4 egg whites

4 tsp olive oil

1 oz/25 g arugula leaves

fresh thyme sprigs, to garnish

NUTRITION

Calories 146	Sugars 2g
Protein 10g	Fat 11g
Carbohydrate 2g	Saturates 2g

1 Halve the tomatoes and place
them in a pan. Wipe the
mushrooms with paper towels, then
trim if necessary, and slice if large.
Place the mushrooms in the pan with
the tomatoes.

2 Add the stock and the bunch of
thyme to the pan. Bring to a boil,
then reduce the heat and simmer,
covered, for 5–6 minutes, or until
tender. Drain, remove the thyme, and
discard. Keep the mixture warm.

3 Meanwhile, whisk the egg yolks
with the water until frothy. Whisk
the 8 egg whites in a clean, greasefree
bowl until stiff and dry.

4 Spoon the egg yolk mixture into
the egg whites and, using a metal
spoon, fold together until well mixed.
Take care not to knock out too much
of the air.

5 Preheat the broiler to medium.
For each omelet, brush a small
omelet pan with 1 teaspoon of the
oil and heat until hot. Pour in a fourth
of the egg mixture and cook for
4–5 minutes, or until the mixture
has set.

6 Finish cooking the omelet under
the hot broiler for 2–3 minutes.

7 Transfer the omelet to a warmed
serving plate. Fill the omelet with
a few arugula leaves and a fourth of
the mushroom and tomato mixture.
Flip over the top of the omelet, then
garnish with thyme sprigs and serve.

spinach cheese molds

serves four

3½ oz/100 g fresh spinach leaves

1⅓ cups skim milk soft cheese

2 garlic cloves, crushed

fresh parsley, tarragon, and chive

    sprigs, finely chopped

salt and pepper

mixed salad greens and fresh herbs,

    to serve

NUTRITION	
Calories 119	Sugars 2g
Protein 6g	Fat 9g
Carbohydrate 2g	Saturates 6g

1 Trim the stems from the spinach leaves and rinse the leaves under cold running water. Pack the leaves into a pan while they are still wet, then cover and cook over medium heat for 3–4 minutes, or until wilted—they will cook in the steam from the wet leaves (do not overcook). Drain well and pat dry with paper towels.

2 Line the bottoms of 4 small ovenproof bowls or individual ramekin dishes with parchment paper. Line the dishes with the spinach leaves so that the leaves overhang the edges.

3 Place the cheese in a bowl and add the garlic and herbs. Mix together thoroughly and season to taste with salt and pepper.

4 Spoon the cheese and herb mixture into the dishes and pull over the overlapping spinach to cover the cheese, or lay extra leaves to cover the top. Place a waxed paper circle on top of each dish and weigh down with a 3½ oz/100 g weight. Let chill in the refrigerator for 1 hour.

5 Remove the weights and peel off the paper. Loosen the molds gently by running a small spatula around the edges of each dish and turn them out onto individual serving plates. Serve immediately with a mixture of salad greens and fresh herbs.

figs & prosciutto

serves four

1½ oz/40 g arugula leaves

4 fresh figs

4 slices prosciutto

4 tbsp olive oil

1 tbsp fresh orange juice

1 tbsp clear honey

1 small fresh red chili

1 Tear the arugula leaves into manageable pieces and arrange on 4 individual serving plates.

2 Using a sharp knife, cut each of the figs into fourths and place them on top of the arugula.

3 Using a sharp knife, cut the prosciutto into strips and sprinkle over the arugula and figs.

4 Place the oil, orange juice, and honey in a screw-top jar. Shake the jar vigorously until the mixture emulsifies and forms a thick dressing. Transfer the dressing to a bowl.

5 Using a sharp knife, dice the chili. (You can remove the seeds first if you prefer a milder flavor.) Add the diced chili to the dressing and mix well.

6 Drizzle the dressing over the prosciutto, arugula, and figs, tossing to mix well. Serve immediately.

COOK'S TIP

Fresh chilies can burn the skin for several hours after chopping, so it is advisable to wear gloves when you are handling any very hot varieties and to wash your hands afterward.

NUTRITION

Calories 121	Sugars 6g
Protein 1g	Fat 11g
Carbohydrate 6g	Saturates 2g

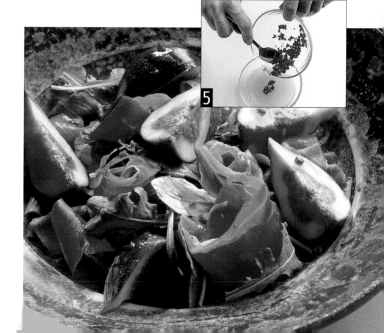

eggplant & rice rolls

serves four

3 eggplants (about 1 lb 10 oz/
750 g in total)

generous ¼ cup mixed long-grain
and wild rice

4 scallions, thinly sliced

3 tbsp chopped cashew nuts or
toasted chopped hazelnuts

2 tbsp capers, drained and rinsed

1 garlic clove, crushed

2 tbsp freshly grated
Parmesan cheese

1 egg, beaten

salt and pepper

1 tbsp olive oil, plus extra
for oiling

1 tbsp balsamic vinegar

2 tbsp tomato paste

⅔ cup water

⅔ cup dry white wine

cilantro sprigs, to garnish

NUTRITION

Calories 142	Sugars 3g
Protein 6g	Fat 9g
Carbohydrate 9g	Saturates 3g

1 Preheat the oven to 350°F/180°C. Cut off the stem end of each eggplant, then cut off and discard a strip of skin from alternate sides of each eggplant. Cut each eggplant into thin slices to give a total of 16 slices.

2 Blanch the eggplant slices in boiling water for 5 minutes, then drain on paper towels.

3 Cook the rice in boiling salted water for 12 minutes, or until just tender. Drain and place in a bowl. Add the scallions, nuts, capers, garlic, cheese, egg, and salt and pepper to taste and stir well.

4 Spread a thin layer of rice mixture over each slice of eggplant and roll up, securing with a wooden toothpick. Place the rolls in an oiled flameproof dish and brush each one with oil.

5 Mix the vinegar, tomato paste, and water together. Pour over the rolls. Cook in the oven for 40 minutes, or until tender and most of the liquid has been absorbed. Transfer to a dish.

6 Add the wine to the pan juices and heat until the sediment loosens, then simmer for 2–3 minutes. Taste and adjust the seasoning if necessary and strain the sauce over the eggplant rolls. Let stand until cold, then chill thoroughly.

7 Garnish the eggplant rolls with cilantro sprigs and serve.

crispy pork & peanut baskets

serves four

2 sheets phyllo pastry, each about
   16½ x 11 inches/42 x 28 cm

2 tbsp vegetable oil

1 garlic clove, crushed

generous 1 cup ground pork

1 tsp Thai red curry paste

2 scallions, finely chopped

3 tbsp chunky peanut butter

1 tbsp light soy sauce

1 tbsp chopped cilantro

salt and pepper

cilantro sprigs, to garnish

COOK'S TIP

When using phyllo pastry, remember that it dries out very quickly and becomes brittle and difficult to handle. Work quickly and keep any sheets you're not using covered with plastic wrap and a dampened dish towel.

NUTRITION

Calories 243	Sugars 1g
Protein 12g	Fat 16g
Carbohydrate 12g	Saturates 3g

1 Preheat the oven to 400°F/200°C. Cut each sheet of phyllo pastry into 24 squares, 2¾ inches/7 cm across, to make a total of 48 squares. Brush each square lightly with oil, and arrange the squares in stacks of 4 in 12 small tartlet pans, pointing outward. Press the pastry down into the pans.

2 Bake the pastry shells in the preheated oven for 6–8 minutes, or until golden brown.

3 Meanwhile, heat the remaining oil in a preheated wok. Add the garlic and fry for 30 seconds, then stir in the pork and stir-fry over high heat for 4–5 minutes, or until the meat is golden brown.

4 Add the curry paste and scallions and stir-fry for an additional 1 minute, then stir in the peanut butter, soy sauce, and chopped cilantro. Season to taste with salt and pepper.

5 Spoon the pork mixture into the phyllo baskets and serve hot, garnished with cilantro sprigs.

crispy golden seafood

serves four

7 oz/200 g prepared squid

7 oz/200 g raw jumbo shrimp,
    shelled and deveined

5½ oz/150 g whitebait

1¼ cups oil, for deep-frying

⅓ cup all-purpose flour

salt and pepper

1 tsp dried basil

Garlic Mayonnaise, to serve
    (see Cook's Tip)

COOK'S TIP

To make the Garlic Mayonnaise,
crush 2 garlic cloves and stir into
8 tablespoons of mayonnaise,
then season to taste with salt
and pepper and 1 tablespoon of
chopped fresh parsley. Cover and
chill in the refrigerator until ready
to serve.

NUTRITION

Calories 393	Sugars 0.2g
Protein 27g	Fat 26g
Carbohydrate 12g	Saturates 3g

1 Carefully rinse the squid, shrimp, and whitebait under cold running water, completely removing any accumulated dirt or grit.

2 Using a sharp knife, slice the squid into thick rings, but leave all the tentacles whole.

3 Heat the oil in a large pan to 350–375°F/180–190°C, or until a cube of bread browns in 30 seconds.

4 Place the flour in a large bowl and season to taste with salt, pepper, and the dried basil.

5 Toss the squid, shrimp, and whitebait in the seasoned flour until coated thoroughly all over. Carefully shake off any excess flour.

6 Cook the seafood, in batches, in the hot oil for 2–3 minutes, or until crispy and golden all over. Remove each batch of seafood with a slotted spoon and let drain thoroughly on paper towels.

7 Transfer the deep-fried seafood to 4 large serving plates and serve immediately with the Garlic Mayonnaise (see Cook's Tip).

steamed crab cakes

serves four

1–2 banana leaves

2 garlic cloves, crushed

1 tsp finely chopped lemongrass

½ tsp pepper

2 tbsp chopped cilantro

3 tbsp creamed coconut

1 tbsp lime juice

7 oz/200 g cooked crabmeat, flaked

1 tbsp Thai fish sauce

2 egg whites

1 egg yolk, lightly beaten

8 cilantro leaves

corn oil, for deep-frying

chili sauce, to serve

NUTRITION

Calories 156	Sugars 1g
Protein 13g	Fat 11g
Carbohydrate 2g	Saturates 4g

1 Line 8 ½-cup ramekin dishes or foil containers with the banana leaves, cutting them to shape.

2 Mix the garlic, lemongrass, pepper, and cilantro together in a bowl. Mash the creamed coconut with the lime juice in a separate bowl until smooth. Stir the 2 mixtures together and add the crabmeat and fish sauce.

3 Whisk the egg whites in a clean, greasefree bowl until stiff, then lightly and evenly fold them into the crab mixture.

4 Spoon the mixture into the prepared ramekin dishes and press down lightly. Brush the tops with egg yolk and top each with a cilantro leaf.

5 Place in a steamer half-filled with boiling water, then cover with a close-fitting lid and steam for 15 minutes, or until firm to the touch. Pour off the excess liquid and remove from the ramekin dishes.

6 Heat the oil in a large pan to 350°–375°F/180–190°C, or until a cube of bread browns in 30 seconds. Add the crab cakes and deep-fry for 1 minute, turning them over once, until golden brown. Serve hot with chili sauce.

sardines with pesto

serves four

16 large sardines, cleaned and scaled

scant 1 cup fresh basil leaves

2 garlic cloves, crushed

2 tbsp pine nuts, toasted

½ cup freshly grated
Parmesan cheese

⅔ cup olive oil

salt and pepper

lemon wedges, to garnish

NUTRITION

Calories 617	Sugars 0g
Protein 27g	Fat 56g
Carbohydrate 1g	Saturates 11g

1 Preheat the broiler. Wash the sardines and pat dry with paper towels. Arrange them on a broiler pan.

2 Place the basil leaves, garlic, and pine nuts in a food processor and process until finely chopped. Transfer to a small bowl and stir in the Parmesan cheese and oil. Season to taste with salt and pepper.

3 Spread a little of the pesto over one side of the sardines and place under the hot broiler for 3 minutes. Turn the fish and spread with more pesto. Broil for an additional 3 minutes, or until the fish are cooked through.

4 Serve the sardines immediately with extra pesto and garnished with lemon wedges.

VARIATION

This treatment will also work well with other small oily fish, such as herrings and sprats.

wild rice blinis

serves four–six

butter or vegetable oil, for frying

4 scallions, thinly sliced diagonally

4 oz/115 g smoked salmon,
   thinly sliced into strips
   or shredded

½ cup sour cream

snipped fresh chives, for sprinkling

BLINIS

5 tbsp lukewarm water

1½ tsp active dry yeast

generous ⅓ cup all-purpose flour

scant ½ cup buckwheat flour

2 tbsp sugar

½ tsp salt

1 cup milk

2 eggs, separated

2 tbsp butter, melted

generous 1 cup cooked wild rice

TO GARNISH

orange twist

fresh mint sprig

1 To make the blinis, pour the water into a small bowl and sprinkle the yeast over it. Let stand until the yeast has dissolved and the mixture is beginning to froth.

2 Sift the flours into a bowl and stir in the sugar and salt. Make a well in the center. Warm ¾ cup of the milk and add to the well with the yeast mixture. Gradually whisk the flour into the liquid to form a smooth batter. Cover and let stand in a warm place until light and bubbly.

3 Beat the remaining milk with the egg yolks and the melted butter, then beat into the batter.

4 Using an electric mixer, whisk the egg whites until soft peaks form. Fold a spoonful into the batter, then fold in the remaining egg whites and the rice alternately. Do not overmix.

5 Heat just enough butter in a large skillet to coat lightly. Drop tablespoonfuls of the batter into the pan and cook for 1–2 minutes, or until tiny bubbles form on the surface. Turn and cook for 30 seconds. Remove and keep warm in a low oven while cooking the remaining batter. Add a little more butter if necessary.

6 Top with the scallions, smoked salmon, sour cream, and a sprinkling of snipped chives. Garnish with an orange twist and mint sprig and serve.

NUTRITION	
Calories 37	Sugars 1g
Protein 1g	Fat 2g
Carbohydrate 4g	Saturates 1g

bang-bang chicken

serves four

4 cups water

2 chicken quarters

1 cucumber, cut into
    short thin sticks

SAUCE

2 tbsp light soy sauce

1 tsp sugar

1 tbsp finely chopped scallions, plus
    extra to garnish

1 tsp red chili oil

¼ tsp pepper

1 tsp white sesame seeds, plus
    extra to garnish

2 tbsp peanut butter, creamed with
    a little sesame oil

NUTRITION

Calories 82	Sugars 1g
Protein 13g	Fat 3g
Carbohydrate 2g	Saturates 1g

1 Bring the water to a rolling boil in a large pan. Add the chicken pieces, then reduce the heat and cook, covered, for 30–35 minutes.

2 Remove the chicken from the pan and immerse in a bowl of cold water for at least 1 hour, to cool it ready for shredding.

3 Remove the chicken pieces and drain, then dry on paper towels. Take the meat off the bone.

4 Pound the chicken with a rolling pin on a flat surface, then tear the meat into shreds with 2 forks. Mix the chicken with the cucumber and arrange in a serving dish.

5 To serve, mix all the sauce ingredients together until thoroughly combined and pour over the chicken and cucumber in the serving dish. Sprinkle some sesame seeds and chopped scallions over the sauce and serve.

COOK'S TIP

Take the time to tear the chicken meat into similar-size shreds, to make an elegant-looking dish. You can do this quite efficiently with 2 forks, although Chinese cooks would do it with their fingers.

turkey & vegetable loaf

serves six

1 onion, finely chopped

1 garlic clove, crushed

2 lb/900 g ground lean turkey

1 tbsp chopped fresh parsley

1 tbsp snipped fresh chives

1 tbsp chopped fresh tarragon

salt and pepper

1 egg white, lightly beaten

2 zucchini, 1 medium and 1 large

2 tomatoes

tomato and herb sauce, to serve
    (optional)

NUTRITION

Calories 165	Sugars 1g
Protein 36g	Fat 2g
Carbohydrate 1g	Saturates 0.5g

COOK'S TIP

To test if the loaf is cooked, insert a skewer into the center—the juices should run clear. The loaf will also shrink away from the sides of the pan.

1 Preheat the oven to 375°F/190°C. Line a nonstick loaf pan with parchment paper. Place the onion, garlic, and turkey in a bowl, then add the herbs and season to taste with salt and pepper. Mix together with your hands, then add the egg white to bind the mixture together.

2 Press half the turkey mixture into the bottom of the pan. Thinly slice the medium zucchini and the tomatoes and arrange the slices over the meat. Top with the rest of the turkey mixture and press down firmly. Cover with a layer of foil and place in a roasting pan. Pour in enough boiling water to come halfway up the sides of the loaf pan. Bake in the oven for 1–1¼ hours, removing the foil for the last 20 minutes of cooking.

3 Cut the large zucchini lengthwise into thin slices with a vegetable peeler. Bring a pan of water to a boil and blanch the zucchini for 1–2 minutes, or until just tender. Drain and keep warm.

4 Remove the loaf from the pan and transfer to a warmed serving platter. Drape the zucchini ribbons over the turkey loaf and serve with a tomato and herb sauce, if desired.

asian pork balls in broth

serves six

1¾ quarts chicken stock
3 oz/85 g shiitake mushrooms,
    thinly sliced
6 oz/175 g bok choy or other
    Chinese greens, sliced into
    thin ribbons
6 scallions, finely sliced
salt and pepper

PORK BALLS

8 oz/225 g ground lean pork
1 oz/25 g fresh spinach leaves,
    finely chopped
2 scallions, finely chopped
1 garlic clove, very finely chopped
pinch of Chinese five-spice powder
1 tsp soy sauce

NUTRITION

Calories 67	Sugars 1g
Protein 9g	Fat 2g
Carbohydrate 3g	Saturates 1g

1 To make the pork balls, place the pork, spinach, scallions, and garlic in a bowl. Add the five-spice powder and soy sauce and mix until thoroughly combined.

2 Shape the pork mixture into 24 balls. Place them in a single layer in a steamer that will fit over the top of a large pan.

3 Bring the stock just to a boil in a pan that will accommodate the steamer. Reduce the heat so that the liquid just bubbles gently. Add the mushrooms to the stock and place the steamer, covered, on top of the pan. Steam for 10 minutes. Remove the steamer and let stand on a plate.

4 Add the bok choy and scallions to the pan and cook gently in the stock for 3–4 minutes, or until the leaves are wilted. Season the broth to taste with salt and pepper.

5 Divide the pork balls evenly between 6 warmed serving bowls and ladle the soup over them. Serve immediately.

spare ribs

serves four

2 lb/900 g pork spare ribs

2 tbsp dark soy sauce

3 tbsp hoisin sauce

1 tbsp rice wine or dry sherry

pinch of Chinese five-spice
   powder

2 tsp brown sugar

¼ tsp chili sauce

2 garlic cloves, crushed

cilantro sprigs, to garnish
   (optional)

NUTRITION

Calories 436	Sugars 3g
Protein 21g	Fat 37g
Carbohydrate 3g	Saturates 14g

1 Cut the spare ribs into separate pieces if they are joined together. If desired, you can chop them into 2-inch/5-cm lengths using a cleaver.

2 Mix the soy sauce, hoisin sauce, rice wine, five-spice powder, sugar, chili sauce, and garlic together in a large bowl.

3 Place the ribs in a shallow dish and pour the mixture over them, turning to coat the ribs thoroughly. Cover with plastic wrap and let marinate in the refrigerator, turning the ribs occasionally, for at least 1 hour.

4 Preheat the oven to 350°F/180°C. Remove the ribs from the marinade and arrange them in a single layer on a wire rack placed over a roasting pan half-filled with warm water. Using a pastry brush, coat the ribs with the marinade, reserving the remaining marinade.

5 Cook the ribs in the preheated oven for 30 minutes. Remove the roasting pan from the oven and turn the ribs over. Brush with the remaining marinade and return to the oven for an additional 30 minutes, or until cooked through. Add more hot water to the roasting pan during cooking, if required. Do not let it dry out, because the water steams the ribs and aids in their cooking.

6 Transfer the ribs to a warmed serving dish. Garnish with cilantro sprigs, if using, and serve immediately.

Snacks & Side Dishes

Vegetables in their wealth of different forms are rich in essential nutrients, and the more varieties you eat, the greater the range of these health-promoting vitamins and minerals you can benefit from. The following recipes take the pick of the crop and, using a range of cooking methods and seasonings, turn them into truly exciting and tempting dishes—perfect for serving with broiled or grilled meat, poultry, or fish, or to enjoy on their own as a low-carb filler at any time of day. Try the speedy stir-fried Bok Choy with Crabmeat (see page 70) or the grilled Roast Leeks (see page 75). Alternatively, opt for the slower-paced yet easy Braised Fennel (see page 78).

Salads are another low-carbohydrate mainstay, and offer a feast of fresh flavor and color—like the Grapefruit & Cheese Salad (see page 96), with pink grapefruit and avocado.

sesame seed chutney

serves four

8 tbsp sesame seeds

2 tbsp water

½ bunch of cilantro

3 fresh green chilies, seeded
 and chopped

1 tsp salt

2 tsp lemon juice

chopped fresh red chili,
 to garnish

NUTRITION

Calories 120	Sugars 0g
Protein 4g	Fat 12g
Carbohydrate 0.2g	Saturates 2g

COOK'S TIP

Dry roasting brings out the flavor
of spices and takes just a
few minutes. You will be able to
tell when the spices are ready
because of the wonderful
fragrance that develops. Stir the
spices constantly to ensure that
they do not burn.

1 Place the sesame seeds in a large
heavy-bottom pan and dry roast
them, stirring constantly. Remove from
the heat and let cool.

2 Place the sesame seeds in a
mortar and, using a pestle, grind
to a fine powder, or process in a food
processor.

3 Add the water to the ground
sesame seeds and mix thoroughly
to form a smooth paste.

4 Finely chop the cilantro. Add the
green chilies and cilantro to the
sesame seed paste and grind again.

5 Add the salt and the lemon
juice to the mixture and grind
once again.

6 Transfer the mixture to a small
serving dish. Garnish with
chopped red chili and serve.

okra bhaji

serves four

- 1 tbsp corn oil
- 1 tsp black mustard seeds
- 1 tsp cumin seeds
- 1 tsp ground coriander
- ½ tsp ground turmeric
- 1 fresh green chili, seeded and finely chopped
- 1 red onion, finely sliced
- 2 garlic cloves, crushed
- 1 orange bell pepper, seeded and thinly sliced
- 1 lb 2 oz/500 g okra, blanched
- generous 1 cup vegetable juice
- salt
- ⅔ cup light cream
- 1 tbsp lemon juice

NUTRITION

Calories 173	Sugars 11g
Protein 6g	Fat 11g
Carbohydrate 13g	Saturates 5g

1 Heat the oil in a preheated wok or large heavy-bottom skillet. Add the mustard seeds and cover the wok until they begin to pop.

2 Stir in the cumin seeds, coriander, turmeric, and chili. Stir constantly for 1 minute, or until the spices give off their aroma.

3 Add the onion, garlic, and bell pepper and cook, stirring frequently, for 5 minutes, or until soft.

4 Add the blanched okra to the wok and stir well.

5 Pour in the vegetable juice, then bring to a boil and cook over high heat, stirring occasionally, for 5 minutes.

6 When most of the liquid has evaporated, taste and adjust the seasoning, adding salt if necessary.

7 Add the cream and return to a boil, then continue to cook the mixture over high heat for 12 minutes, or until it is almost dry.

8 Sprinkle the lemon juice over the okra bhaji. Transfer to a warmed serving dish and serve immediately.

vegetables à la grecque

serves four–six

9 oz/250 g small pickling onions

9 oz/250 g mushrooms

9 oz/250 g zucchini

2 cups water

5 tbsp olive oil

2 tbsp lemon juice

2 strips of lemon rind

2 large garlic cloves, thinly sliced

½ Spanish onion, finely chopped

1 bay leaf

15 black peppercorns,
   lightly crushed

10 coriander seeds, lightly crushed

pinch of dried oregano

finely chopped fresh flatleaf parsley
   or cilantro, to garnish

NUTRITION

Calories 67	Sugars 4g
Protein 2g	Fat 4g
Carbohydrate 6g	Saturates 1g

1 Place the pickling onions in a heatproof bowl and cover with boiling water. Let stand for 2 minutes, then drain. Peel and reserve.

2 Trim the mushroom stems. Cut the mushrooms into halves or fourths, or leave whole if small. Cut thin strips of peel from the zucchini for a decorative finish, then cut into ¼-inch/5-mm slices. Reserve the mushrooms and zucchini.

3 Place the water, oil, lemon juice and rind, garlic, Spanish onion, bay leaf, peppercorns, coriander seeds, and oregano in a pan over high heat and bring to a boil. Reduce the heat and simmer for 15 minutes.

4 Add the small onions and simmer for an additional 5 minutes. Add the mushrooms and zucchini and simmer for an additional 2 minutes.

5 Using a slotted spoon, transfer all the vegetables to a large heatproof dish.

6 Return the liquid to a boil and boil until reduced to 6 tablespoons. Pour the liquid over the vegetables and let cool completely.

7 Cover with plastic wrap and let chill for at least 12 hours.

8 To serve, place the vegetables and cooking liquid in a serving dish and sprinkle the fresh herbs over them.

bok choy with crabmeat

serves four

2 heads bok choy, about 9 oz/
    250 g in total

2 tbsp vegetable oil

1 garlic clove, thinly sliced

2 tbsp oyster sauce

3½ oz/100 g cherry tomatoes,
    halved

6 oz/175 g canned white
    crabmeat, drained

salt and pepper

VARIATION

If bok choy is not available,
Napa cabbage makes a good
alternative for this dish.

1 Trim the bok choy and cut into 1-inch/2.5-cm thick slices.

2 Heat the oil in a large skillet or wok. Add the garlic and stir-fry over high heat for 1 minute.

3 Add the bok choy and stir-fry for 2–3 minutes, or until the leaves wilt but the stems are still crisp.

4 Add the oyster sauce and tomatoes and stir-fry for an additional 1 minute.

5 Add the crabmeat and season to taste with salt and pepper. Stir to heat thoroughly and break up the distribution of crabmeat before serving.

NUTRITION

Calories 101	Sugars 2g
Protein 9g	Fat 6g
Carbohydrate 3g	Saturates 1g

stir-fried ginger mushrooms

serves four

2 tbsp vegetable oil

3 garlic cloves, crushed

1 tbsp Thai red curry paste

½ tsp ground turmeric

15 oz/425 g canned straw
    mushrooms, drained and halved

¾-inch/2-cm piece fresh gingerroot,
    finely shredded

generous ⅓ cup coconut milk

1½ oz/40 g dried shiitake
    mushrooms, soaked, drained,
    and sliced

1 tbsp lemon juice

1 tbsp light soy sauce

2 tsp sugar

½ tsp salt

8 cherry tomatoes, halved

7 oz/200 g firm tofu (drained
    weight), diced

cilantro leaves, to garnish

1 Heat the oil in a skillet. Add the garlic and stir-fry for 1 minute. Stir in the curry paste and turmeric and cook for an additional 30 seconds.

2 Stir in the straw mushrooms and ginger and stir-fry for 2 minutes. Stir in the coconut milk and bring to a boil.

3 Stir in the dried shiitake mushrooms, lemon juice, soy sauce, sugar, and salt and heat thoroughly. Add the tomatoes and tofu and toss gently to heat through.

4 Sprinkle the cilantro leaves over the mushroom mixture and serve immediately.

NUTRITION	
Calories 174	Sugars 7g
Protein 8g	Fat 9g
Carbohydrate 15g	Saturates 1g

brindil bhaji

serves four

1 lb 2 oz/500 g eggplants, sliced

2 tbsp vegetable oil or ghee

1 onion, thinly sliced

2 garlic cloves, sliced

1-inch/2.5-cm piece fresh
    gingerroot, grated

½ tsp ground turmeric

1 dried red chili, finely chopped

½ tsp salt

14 oz/400 g canned tomatoes

1 tsp garam masala

cilantro sprigs, to garnish

NUTRITION

Calories 117	Sugars 8g
Protein 3g	Fat 8g
Carbohydrate 9g	Saturates 5g

VARIATION

Other vegetables can be used
instead of the eggplants. Try
zucchini, potatoes, or bell
peppers, or any combination of
these vegetables, using the
same sauce.

1 Cut the eggplant slices into finger-
width strips.

2 Heat the oil in a heavy-bottom
pan. Add the onion and cook
over medium heat, stirring constantly,
for 7–8 minutes, or until very soft and
just beginning to color.

3 Add the garlic and eggplant
strips, then increase the heat and
cook, stirring constantly, for 2 minutes.
Stir in the ginger, turmeric, chili, salt,
and tomatoes with their can juices.
Use the back of a wooden spoon to
break up the tomatoes. Reduce the
heat and let simmer, uncovered, for
15–20 minutes, or until the eggplants
are very soft.

4 Stir in the garam masala and
simmer for an additional
4–5 minutes.

5 Transfer the brindil bhaji to
a warmed serving plate and
garnish with cilantro sprigs, then
serve immediately.

roasted vegetables

serves six

1 small red cabbage

1 fennel bulb

1 orange bell pepper, cut into
1½-inch/4-cm dice

1 eggplant, halved and sliced into
½-inch/1-cm pieces

2 zucchini, thickly sliced
diagonally

6 fresh rosemary twigs, about
6 inches/15 cm long, soaked in
cold water

olive oil, for brushing

salt and pepper

NUTRITION

Calories 16	Sugars 3g
Protein 1g	Fat 0.3g
Carbohydrate 3g	Saturates 0g

1 Preheat the broiler or grill. Cut the red cabbage through the middle of its stem and heart. Divide each piece into fourths, each time including a section of the stem in the slice to hold it together.

2 Prepare the fennel in the same way as the red cabbage.

3 Blanch the red cabbage and fennel in boiling water for 3 minutes, then drain well.

4 With a wooden skewer, carefully pierce a hole through the middle of each piece of vegetable.

5 Thread a piece of bell pepper, fennel, red cabbage, eggplant, and zucchini onto each rosemary twig, gently pushing the rosemary through the skewer holes.

6 Brush liberally with oil and season with plenty of salt and pepper.

7 Cook under the hot broiler or over hot coals for 8–10 minutes, turning occasionally. Serve.

VARIATION

If you are using a grill, fruit skewers make a quick and easy dessert. Thread pieces of banana, mango, peach, strawberry, apple, and pear onto soaked wooden skewers and cook over the dying embers. Brush with sugar syrup toward the end of cooking.

tomato sauce

serves four

1 tbsp olive oil

1 small onion, chopped

1 garlic clove, crushed

7 oz/200 g canned chopped
   tomatoes

2 tsp tomato paste

½ tsp sugar

½ tsp dried oregano

1 bay leaf

salt and pepper

NUTRITION

Calories 41	Sugars 3g
Protein 1g	Fat 3g
Carbohydrate 3g	Saturates 0.4g

1 Heat the oil in a pan. Add the onion and garlic and cook for 5 minutes until soft but not browned.

2 Add the tomatoes, tomato paste, sugar, oregano, bay leaf, and salt and pepper to taste. Stir well.

3 Bring the sauce to a boil, then cover and let simmer gently for 20 minutes, stirring occasionally, until you have a thickish sauce.

4 Remove the bay leaf and season to taste with salt and pepper. Let cool completely before using. This sauce keeps well in a screw-top jar in the refrigerator for up to 1 week.

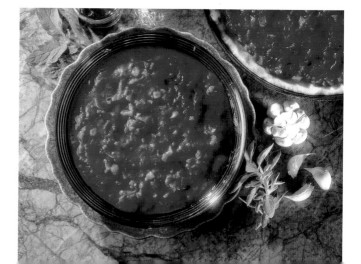

roast leeks

serves four

4 leeks

3 tbsp olive oil

2 tsp balsamic vinegar

sea salt and pepper

NUTRITION

Calories 71	Sugars 2g
Protein 2g	Fat 6g
Carbohydrate 3g	Saturates 1g

COOK'S TIP

Use a good quality French or Italian olive oil for this deliciously simple yet sophisticated vegetable accompaniment.

1 Preheat the grill. Cut the leeks in half lengthwise, making sure that you hold the knife straight, so that the leek is held together by the root. Brush each leek liberally with oil.

2 Cook the leeks over hot coals for 6–7 minutes, turning once.

3 Remove the leeks from the grill and brush them lightly with the vinegar.

4 Season to taste with salt and pepper and serve hot or warm.

sweet & sour zucchini

serves four–six

1 lb 2 oz/500 g zucchini

3 tbsp olive oil

1 large garlic clove, finely chopped

3 tbsp white wine vinegar

3 tbsp water

6–8 anchovy fillets, canned
  or salted

3 tbsp pine nuts

3 tbsp raisins

salt and pepper

fresh flatleaf parsley sprigs,
  to garnish

VARIATION

Replace the raisins with golden raisins. Add a little grated lemon or orange rind for added zing.

---

1 Cut the zucchini into long thin strips. Heat the oil in a large heavy-bottom skillet over medium heat. Add the garlic and cook, stirring constantly, for 2 minutes.

2 Add the zucchini and cook, stirring frequently, until they just begin to turn brown. Add the vinegar and water. Reduce the heat and simmer for 10 minutes.

3 Meanwhile, drain the anchovies, if canned, or rinse if they are salted. Coarsely chop, then use the back of a wooden spoon to mash them to a paste.

4 Stir the anchovies, pine nuts, and raisins into the skillet. Increase the heat and stir until the zucchini are coated in a thin sauce and are tender. Taste and adjust the seasoning, remembering that the anchovies are very salty.

5 Either serve immediately or let cool completely, then serve at room temperature. To serve, garnish with parsley sprigs.

NUTRITION

Calories 90	Sugars 5g
Protein 3g	Fat 4g
Carbohydrate 5g	Saturates 1g

braised fennel

serves four–six

2 lemon slices

3 fennel bulbs

4½ tsp olive oil

3 tbsp butter

4 fresh thyme sprigs or ½ tbsp

 dried thyme

pepper

¾ cup chicken or vegetable stock

¾ cup freshly grated

 Parmesan cheese

NUTRITION

Calories 149	Sugars 2g
Protein 6g	Fat 13g
Carbohydrate 2g	Saturates 7g

1 Preheat the oven to 400°F/200°C. Bring a pan of water to a boil and add the lemon slices. Slice the fennel lengthwise and add to the pan. Return the water to a boil, then reduce the heat and simmer for 8 minutes, or until just tender. Drain.

2 Place the oil and butter in a flameproof casserole over medium heat. Swirl the melted mixture around so the bottom and sides of the casserole are well coated.

COOK'S TIP

This is an ideal way to serve older fennel bulbs, but will not improve any that have been stored too long and dried out.

3 Add the fennel slices and stir until coated. Add the thyme and season to taste with pepper. Pour in the stock and sprinkle the Parmesan cheese over the top.

4 Bake in the preheated oven for 25–30 minutes, or until the fennel has absorbed the stock and is tender and the cheese has melted and become golden brown. Serve immediately.

steamed lotus rice

serves four

2 lotus leaves

4 dried shiitake mushrooms

generous ¾ cup long-grain rice

1 cinnamon stick

6 cardamom pods

4 cloves

1 tsp salt

2 eggs

1 tbsp vegetable oil

2 scallions, chopped

1 tbsp soy sauce

2 tbsp sherry

1 tsp sugar

1 tsp sesame oil

NUTRITION

Calories 163	Sugars 0.1g
Protein 5g	Fat 6g
Carbohydrate 2.1g	Saturates 1g

1 Unfold the lotus leaves and cut along the fold to divide each leaf in half. Lay on a cookie sheet and pour over enough hot water to cover. Let soak for 30 minutes, or until softened.

2 Meanwhile, place the mushrooms in a bowl, then cover with warm water and let soak for 20–25 minutes.

3 Bring a pan of water to a boil. Add the rice, cinnamon stick, cardamoms, cloves, and salt and return to a boil, then cook for 10 minutes— the rice should be partially cooked. Drain well and remove the cinnamon stick. Place the rice in a bowl.

4 Beat the eggs lightly in a separate bowl. Heat the vegetable oil in a preheated wok and cook the eggs quickly, stirring until set. Remove and reserve.

5 Drain the mushrooms, squeezing out the excess water. Remove the tough stems and chop the mushrooms. Stir into the rice with the egg, scallions, soy sauce, sherry, sugar, and sesame oil.

6 Drain the lotus leaves and divide the rice into 4 portions. Place a portion in the center of each leaf and fold up to form a package. Place in a steamer, then cover and steam over simmering water for 20 minutes. To serve, cut the tops of the lotus leaves open to expose the rice inside.

bamboo with spinach

serves four

3 tbsp peanut oil

8 oz/225 g fresh spinach, chopped

6 oz/175 g canned bamboo shoots, drained and rinsed

1 garlic clove, crushed

2 fresh red chilies, sliced

pinch of ground cinnamon

1¼ cups vegetable stock

pinch of sugar

pinch of salt

1 tbsp light soy sauce

NUTRITION

Calories 105	Sugars 1g
Protein 3g	Fat 9g
Carbohydrate 3g	Saturates 2g

COOK'S TIP

Fresh bamboo shoots are rarely available in the West. Canned bamboo shoots are quite satisfactory, because they are used to provide a crunchy texture, rather than for their flavor, which is quite bland.

1 Heat the oil in a preheated wok or large heavy-bottom skillet, swirling the oil around the bottom of the wok until it is very hot.

2 Add the spinach and bamboo shoots to the wok and stir-fry for 1 minute.

3 Add the garlic, chilies, and cinnamon to the wok and stir-fry for an additional 30 seconds.

4 Stir in the stock, sugar, salt, and soy sauce, then cover and cook over medium heat for 5 minutes, or until the vegetables are cooked through and the sauce has reduced. (If there is too much cooking liquid, blend a little cornstarch with double the quantity of cold water and stir it into the sauce.) Transfer the bamboo shoots and spinach to a serving dish and serve.

easy cauliflower & broccoli

2 baby cauliflowers

8 oz/225 g broccoli

salt and pepper

SAUCE

8 tbsp olive oil

4 tbsp butter or margarine

2 tsp grated fresh gingerroot

juice and rind of 2 lemons

5 tbsp chopped cilantro

5 tbsp grated Cheddar cheese

COOK'S TIP

Lime or orange could be used instead of the lemon for a fruity and refreshing sauce.

---

1 Preheat the broiler. Cut the cauliflowers in half and the broccoli into very large florets.

2 Cook the cauliflower and broccoli in a pan of boiling salted water for 10 minutes. Drain well, then transfer to a shallow ovenproof dish and keep warm until required.

3 To make the sauce, place the oil and butter in a skillet and heat gently until the butter melts.

NUTRITION	
Calories 433	Sugars 2g
Protein 8g	Fat 44g
Carbohydrate 3g	Saturates 9g

4 Add the ginger, lemon juice and rind, and chopped cilantro and simmer for 2–3 minutes, stirring occasionally.

5 Season the sauce to taste with salt and pepper, then pour over the vegetables in the dish and sprinkle the cheese on top.

6 Cook under the hot broiler for 2–3 minutes, or until the cheese is bubbling and golden brown. Let cool for 1–2 minutes, then serve.

mushroom salad

serves four

5½ oz/150 g firm white mushrooms

4 tbsp virgin olive oil

1 tbsp lemon juice

5 canned anchovy fillets, drained
and chopped

salt and pepper

1 tbsp fresh marjoram, to garnish

NUTRITION

Calories 121	Sugars 0.1g
Protein 13g	Fat 13g
Carbohydrate 0.1g	Saturates 2g

COOK'S TIP

Do not season the mushroom salad with salt until the very last minute, because it will cause the mushrooms to blacken and the juices to leak. The result will not be so tasty, because the full flavors won't be absorbed, and it will also look very unattractive.

1 Gently wipe each mushroom with a damp cloth or damp paper towels in order to remove any dirt.

2 Using a sharp knife, thinly slice the mushrooms and place in a bowl.

3 To make the dressing, whisk the oil and lemon juice together in a small bowl.

4 Pour the dressing mixture over the mushrooms. Toss together so that the mushrooms are completely coated with the lemon juice and oil.

5 Stir the anchovy fillets into the mushrooms. Season the mixture to taste with pepper and garnish with the marjoram.

6 Let the mushroom salad stand at room temperature for 5 minutes before serving to let all the flavors be absorbed.

7 Season the mushroom salad with a little salt (see Cook's Tip), then serve immediately.

mixed leaf salad

serves four

½ head frisée

½ head oak leaf lettuce

few leaves of radicchio

1 head Belgian endive

1 oz/25 g arugula leaves

few fresh basil or flatleaf
    parsley sprigs

edible flowers, to garnish
    (optional)

FRENCH DRESSING

1 tbsp white wine vinegar

pinch of sugar

½ tsp Dijon mustard

3 tbsp extra virgin olive oil

salt and pepper

COOK'S TIP

Violets, hardy geraniums, nasturtiums, chive flowers, and pot marigolds add vibrant colors and a sweet flavor to this salad. Use it as a centerpiece at a dinner party, or to liven up a simple everyday meal.

---

1 Tear the frisée, oak leaf lettuce, and radicchio into pieces. Place the salad greens in a large serving bowl or individual bowls, if you prefer.

2 Cut the Belgian endive into diagonal slices and add to the bowl with the arugula and basil.

3 To make the dressing, beat the vinegar, sugar, and mustard together in a small bowl until the sugar has dissolved. Gradually beat in the oil until the dressing is creamy and thoroughly mixed. Season to taste with salt and pepper.

4 Pour the dressing over the salad and toss thoroughly. Sprinkle a mixture of edible flowers over the top and serve.

NUTRITION	
Calories 51	Sugars 0.1g
Protein 0.1g	Fat 6g
Carbohydrate 1g	Saturates 0.4g

sesame seed salad

serves four

1 large eggplant

salt and pepper

3 tbsp sesame seed paste

juice and rind of 1 lemon

1 garlic clove, crushed

pinch of paprika

1 tbsp chopped cilantro

Boston lettuce leaves

TO GARNISH

pimiento strips

lemon wedges

toasted sesame seeds

NUTRITION

Calories 89	Sugars 1g
Protein 3g	Fat 8g
Carbohydrate 1g	Saturates 1g

1 Cut the eggplant in half, then place in a colander and sprinkle with salt. Let stand for 30 minutes so that the juices drain. Rinse thoroughly under cold running water and drain well. Pat dry with paper towels.

2 Preheat the oven to 450°F/ 230°C. Place the eggplant halves, skin-side uppermost, on an oiled cookie sheet. Cook in the preheated oven for 10–15 minutes. Let cool.

3 When the eggplant halves are cool enough to handle, cut them into cubes and reserve until required.

4 Mix the sesame seed paste, lemon juice and rind, garlic, paprika, and cilantro together in a medium-size bowl. Season to taste with salt and pepper and stir in the eggplant cubes.

5 Line a serving dish with lettuce leaves and spoon the eggplant cubes into the center. Garnish the salad with pimiento slices, lemon wedges, and toasted sesame seeds and serve immediately.

cool cucumber salad

serves four

8 oz/225 g cucumber

1 fresh green chili, finely chopped
(optional)

DRESSING

cilantro leaves, finely chopped

2 tbsp lemon juice

½ tsp salt

1 tsp sugar

TO GARNISH

fresh mint sprigs

red bell pepper strips

COOK'S TIP

For the best results, you can use a vegetable peeler to thinly slice the cucumber.

NUTRITION

Calories 11	Sugars 2g
Protein 0.4g	Fat 0g
Carbohydrate 2g	Saturates 0g

1 Slice the cucumber thinly. Arrange the cucumber slices on a round serving plate.

2 Sprinkle the chili, if using, over the cucumber.

3 To make the dressing, mix the cilantro, lemon juice, salt, and sugar together in a bowl.

4 Cover the cucumber and let chill in the refrigerator for at least 1 hour, or until required. When ready to serve, transfer the cucumber to a serving dish. Pour the salad dressing over the cucumber just before serving and garnish with mint sprigs and red bell pepper strips.

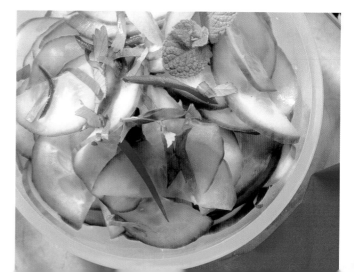

italian mozzarella salad

serves six

7 oz/200 g fresh baby spinach leaves

4½ oz/125 g watercress

4½ oz/125 g mozzarella cheese

8 oz/225 g cherry tomatoes

2 tsp balsamic vinegar

4½ tsp extra virgin olive oil

salt and pepper

NUTRITION	
Calories 79	Sugars 2g
Protein 4g	Fat 6g
Carbohydrate 2g	Saturates 2g

1 Rinse the spinach and watercress under cold running water and drain thoroughly on paper towels. Remove any tough stems. Place the spinach and watercress leaves in a large serving dish.

2 Cut the mozzarella into small pieces and sprinkle them over the spinach and watercress leaves.

3 Cut the tomatoes in half and sprinkle them over the salad.

4 Sprinkle over the vinegar and oil and season to taste with salt and pepper. Toss the mixture together to coat the leaves. Serve immediately or let chill in the refrigerator until required.

lobster salad

serves two

2 raw lobster tails

radicchio leaves

LEMON-DILL MAYONNAISE

1 large lemon

1 large egg yolk

½ tsp Dijon mustard

⅔ cup olive oil

salt and pepper

1 tbsp chopped fresh dill

TO GARNISH

lemon wedges

fresh dill sprigs

NUTRITION

Calories 487		Sugars 2g	
Protein 24g		Fat 42g	
Carbohydrate 2g		Saturates 6g	

1 To make the lemon-dill mayonnaise, finely grate the lemon rind and squeeze the juice. Beat the egg yolk in a small bowl and beat in the mustard and 1 teaspoon of the lemon juice.

2 Using a balloon whisk or electric mixer, beat in the oil, drop by drop, until a thick mayonnaise forms. Stir in half the lemon rind and 1 tablespoon of the juice.

3 Season to taste with salt and pepper and add more lemon juice if desired. Stir in the dill and cover with plastic wrap. Chill in the refrigerator until required.

4 Bring a large pan of lightly salted water to a boil. Add the lobster tails, then return to a boil and cook for 6 minutes, or until the flesh is opaque and the shells are red. Drain immediately and let cool.

5 Remove the lobster flesh from the shells and cut into bite-size pieces. Arrange the radicchio leaves on individual serving plates and top with the lobster flesh. Place a spoonful of the lemon-dill mayonnaise on the side. Garnish with lemon wedges and dill sprigs and serve.

smoked trout & apple salad

serves four

2 orange-red dessert apples

2 tbsp French Dressing
(see page 85)

½ bunch of watercress

1 smoked trout, about 6 oz/175 g

HORSERADISH DRESSING

½ cup lowfat plain yogurt

½–1 tsp lemon juice

1 tbsp horseradish sauce

milk (optional)

salt and pepper

TO GARNISH

1 tbsp snipped fresh chives

fresh chive flowers (optional)

NUTRITION

Calories 133	Sugars 11g
Protein 12g	Fat 5g
Carbohydrate 11g	Saturates 1g

1 Leaving the skin on, cut the apples into fourths and remove the cores. Slice the apples into a bowl and toss in the French Dressing to prevent them turning brown.

2 Break the watercress into sprigs and arrange on 4 serving plates.

3 Skin the trout and take out the bones. Carefully remove any fine bones that remain, using your fingers or tweezers. Flake the trout into fairly large pieces and arrange with the apple between the watercress.

4 To make the Horseradish Dressing, whisk all the ingredients together, adding a little milk if too thick, then drizzle over the trout. Sprinkle the snipped chives and flowers, if using, over the trout and serve.

mozzarella & tomato salad

serves four–six

1 lb/450 g cherry tomatoes

4 scallions

½ cup extra virgin olive oil

2 tbsp balsamic vinegar

salt and pepper

7 oz/200 g buffalo mozzarella (see
Cook's Tip), cut into cubes

scant ¼ cup fresh flatleaf parsley

generous ⅓ cup fresh basil leaves

NUTRITION	
Calories 295	Sugars 3g
Protein 9g	Fat 27g
Carbohydrate 3g	Saturates 7g

1 Using a sharp knife, cut the tomatoes in half and place them in a large bowl. Trim the scallions and finely chop both the green and white parts, then add to the bowl.

2 Pour in the oil and vinegar and use your hands to toss together. Season to taste with salt and pepper, then add the mozzarella and toss again. Cover with plastic wrap and let chill in the refrigerator for 4 hours.

3 Remove the salad from the refrigerator 10 minutes before serving. Finely chop the parsley and add to the salad. Tear the basil leaves and sprinkle them over the salad. Toss all the ingredients together again. Adjust the seasoning and serve.

COOK'S TIP

For the best flavor, buy buffalo mozzarella—*mozzarella di bufala*—rather than the factory-made cow's milk version. This salad would also look good made with bocconcini, which are small balls of mozzarella. Find them in Italian delis.

capri salad

serves four

2 beefsteak tomatoes

4½ oz/125 g mozzarella cheese

12 black olives

8 fresh basil leaves

1 tbsp balsamic vinegar

1 tbsp extra virgin olive oil

salt and pepper

fresh basil leaves, to garnish

NUTRITION

Calories 95	Sugars 3g
Protein 3g	Fat 8g
Carbohydrate 3g	Saturates 3g

COOK'S TIP

Beefsteak tomatoes are excellent both cooked and raw, because they have a good flavor. When buying tomatoes, always look for ones that are firm to the touch and have a bright red color.

1 Preheat the broiler. Cut the tomatoes into thin slices.

2 Drain the mozzarella, if necessary, and cut into slices.

3 Pit the olives and slice them into rings.

4 Layer the tomatoes, mozzarella slices, olives, and basil leaves in a stack, finishing with a layer of cheese on top.

5 Place each stack under the hot broiler for 2–3 minutes, or just long enough to melt the mozzarella.

6 Drizzle over the vinegar and oil and season to taste with salt and pepper.

7 Transfer to individual serving plates and garnish with basil leaves. Serve immediately.

grapefruit & cheese salad

serves four

½ romaine lettuce

½ oak leaf lettuce

2 pink grapefruit

2 ripe avocados

6 oz/175 g Gorgonzola cheese,
   thinly sliced

fresh basil sprigs, to garnish

DRESSING

4 tbsp olive oil

1 tbsp white wine vinegar

salt and pepper

NUTRITION

Calories 390	Sugars 3g	
Protein 13g	Fat 36g	
Carbohydrate 4g	Saturates 13g	

1 Arrange the lettuce leaves on 4 individual serving plates.

2 Remove the peel and pith from the grapefruit with a sharp serrated knife, catching the grapefruit juice in a bowl.

3 Segment the grapefruit by cutting down each side of the membrane. Remove all the membrane. Arrange the segments on the serving plates.

COOK'S TIP

Pink grapefruit segments make a very attractive color combination with the avocados, but ordinary grapefruit will work just as well. To help avocados to ripen, keep them at room temperature in a brown paper bag.

4 Peel, pit, and slice the avocados, dipping them in the grapefruit juice to prevent them turning brown. Arrange the slices on the salad with the cheese.

5 To make the dressing, mix any remaining grapefruit juice, oil, and vinegar together in a bowl. Season to taste with salt and pepper and mix thoroughly to combine.

6 Drizzle the dressing over the salads. Garnish with basil sprigs and serve immediately.

Meat & Poultry

Meat and poultry dishes minus our beloved high-carbohydrate components need not be uninspiring or unsatisfying, as these recipes will soon reveal. Here, plain broils and grills are transformed by first marinating in spices, herbs, and citrus juices, vinegars, or wine, which not only boosts the flavor but also tenderizes the flesh. All that is required is a little advance preparation—the cooking takes just a few minutes.

Other recipes make clever use of stuffings and wrappings, for added flavor interest, such as lean pork stuffed with a Parmesan and basil filling, wrapped in prosciutto, and pieces of tender turkey breast stuffed with soft cheese and sage, wrapped in bacon.

Fruits are also put to creative use in this chapter—ham is paired with spiced apple, duck with piquant raspberries, and chicken with sweet-scented mango.

beef in barolo

serves four

4 tbsp corn oil

2 lb 4 oz/1 kg rolled rib or
    rib-eye roast

2 garlic cloves, crushed

4 shallots, sliced

1 tsp chopped fresh rosemary

1 tsp chopped fresh oregano

2 celery stalks, sliced

1 large carrot, diced

2 whole cloves

1 bottle Barolo wine

freshly grated nutmeg

salt and pepper

cooked vegetables, such as broccoli
    and carrots, to serve

NUTRITION

Calories 744	Sugars 1g
Protein 66g	Fat 43g
Carbohydrate 1g	Saturates 16g

1 Heat the oil in a flameproof casserole and brown the meat all over. Remove the meat from the casserole and reserve.

2 Add the garlic, shallots, herbs, celery, carrot, and cloves to the casserole and cook for 5 minutes.

3 Replace the meat on top of the vegetables. Pour in the wine, then cover and simmer gently for 2 hours, or until tender. Remove the meat from the casserole and let rest before slicing, then keep warm.

4 Press the remaining contents of the casserole through a strainer or process in a food processor, adding a little hot beef stock if necessary. Season to taste with nutmeg, salt, and pepper.

5 Serve the meat with the sauce and accompanied by cooked vegetables, such as broccoli and carrots.

COOK'S TIP

Barolo is a famous wine from the Piedmont area of Italy. If it is unavailable, choose another full-bodied red wine instead.

beef with exotic mushrooms

serves four

4 tenderloin or sirloin steaks

2 tbsp butter

1–2 garlic cloves, crushed

5½ oz/150 g mixed exotic
mushrooms

2 tbsp chopped fresh parsley

TO SERVE

salad greens

cherry tomatoes, halved

NUTRITION

Calories 414		Sugars 0g
Protein 49g		Fat 24g
Carbohydrate 1g		Saturates 13g

COOK'S TIP

Exotic mushrooms, such as shiitake, oyster, and chanterelle, are now readily available in supermarkets. Look for boxes of mixed exotic mushrooms, which are usually cheaper than buying the different types individually.

1 Preheat the grill. Place the steaks on a cutting board and, using a sharp knife, cut a slit in the side of each steak.

2 To make the stuffing, heat the butter in a skillet, then add the garlic and cook gently for 1 minute.

3 Add the mushrooms to the pan and cook for 4–6 minutes, or until tender. Stir in the parsley.

4 Divide the mushroom mixture into fourths and insert a portion into the slit of each steak. Seal the slit closed with a wooden toothpick. If preparing ahead, let the mixture cool before stuffing the steaks.

5 Cook the steaks over hot coals, searing the meat over the hottest part of the grill for 2 minutes on each side. Move the steaks to an area with slightly less intense heat (usually the sides) and cook for an additional 4–10 minutes on each side, depending on how well done you like your steaks.

6 Transfer the steaks to serving plates and remove the toothpicks. Serve the steaks with salad greens and cherry tomatoes.

beef, tomato & olive kabobs

makes eight

1 lb/450 g tenderloin or sirloin steak

16 cherry tomatoes

16 large pitted green olives

salt and pepper

BASTE

4 tbsp olive oil, plus extra for oiling

1 tbsp sherry vinegar

1 garlic clove, crushed

FRESH TOMATO RELISH

1 tbsp olive oil

½ red onion, finely chopped

1 garlic clove, chopped

6 plum tomatoes, peeled, seeded, and chopped

2 pitted green olives, sliced

1 tbsp chopped fresh parsley

1 tbsp lemon juice

1 Preheat the grill. Trim any fat from the beef and cut into 24 pieces.

2 Thread the meat onto 8 presoaked wooden skewers, alternating the pieces with cherry tomatoes and olives.

3 To make the baste, combine the oil, vinegar, garlic, and salt and pepper to taste in a bowl.

4 To make the relish, heat the oil in a small pan. Add the onion and garlic and cook for 3–4 minutes, or until softened. Add the plum tomatoes and olives and cook for 2–3 minutes, or until the tomatoes are softened slightly. Stir in the parsley, lemon juice, and salt and pepper to taste. Reserve.

NUTRITION	
Calories 166	Sugars 1g
Protein 12g	Fat 12g
Carbohydrate 1g	Saturates 3g

5 Cook the skewers on an oiled rack over hot coals for 5–10 minutes, basting and turning frequently. Serve with the relish.

scallops & italian sausage

serves four

1 tbsp olive oil

6 canned anchovy fillets, drained

1 tbsp capers, drained

1 tbsp chopped fresh
    rosemary leaves

finely grated rind and juice of
    1 orange

2¾ oz/75 g Italian sausage,
    diced

3 tomatoes, peeled and chopped

4 turkey or veal scallops, about
    4½ oz/125 g each

salt and pepper

NUTRITION

Calories 233	Sugars 1g
Protein 28g	Fat 13g
Carbohydrate 1g	Saturates 1g

1 Heat the oil in a large skillet. Add the anchovies, capers, rosemary, orange rind and juice, Italian sausage, and tomatoes and cook for 5–6 minutes, stirring occasionally.

2 Meanwhile, place the turkey scallops between sheets of waxed paper. Pound the meat with a meat mallet or the end of a rolling pin to flatten it.

3 Add the meat to the mixture in the skillet. Season to taste with salt and pepper, then cover and cook for 3–5 minutes on each side, slightly longer if the meat is thicker.

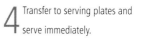

4 Transfer to serving plates and serve immediately.

COOK'S TIP

Try using 4-minute steaks, slightly flattened, instead of the turkey or veal. Cook them for 4–5 minutes on top of the sauce in the skillet.

meatball brochettes

serves four

2½ tbsp bulgur wheat

12 oz/350 g ground lean beef

1 onion, finely chopped (optional)

1 tbsp tomato ketchup

1 tbsp brown fruity sauce

1 tbsp chopped fresh parsley

beaten egg, to bind (optional)

8 cherry tomatoes

8 white mushrooms

vegetable oil, for basting

assorted cooked vegetables,

   to serve

NUTRITION

Calories 120	Sugars 2g
Protein 17g	Fat 5g
Carbohydrate 2g	Saturates 2g

1 Preheat the grill. Place the bulgur wheat in a heatproof bowl and cover with boiling water. Let soak for 20 minutes, or until softened. Drain well and let cool.

2 Place the soaked wheat, beef, onion, if using, ketchup, brown sauce, and parsley together in a large bowl and mix well until all the ingredients are well combined. Add a little beaten egg if necessary to bind the mixture together.

3 Using your hands, shape the meat mixture into 18 even-size balls. Cover and let chill in the refrigerator for 30 minutes.

4 Thread the meatballs onto 8 presoaked wooden skewers, alternating them with the tomatoes and mushrooms.

5 Brush the brochettes with a little oil and cook over hot coals, turning occasionally and brushing with a little more oil if the meat begins to dry out, for 10 minutes, or until cooked through.

6 Transfer to warmed serving plates and serve with vegetables.

ground lamb with peas

serves four

6 tbsp corn oil

1 onion, sliced

2 fresh red chilies, chopped

1 bunch of cilantro, chopped

2 tomatoes, chopped

1 tsp salt

1 tsp finely chopped fresh
  gingerroot

1 garlic clove, crushed

1 tsp chili powder

1 lb/450 g ground lean lamb

scant 1 cup peas

2 fresh green chilies, to garnish

COOK'S TIP

The flavor of garlic varies
in strength depending on how
it is prepared. For instance,
a whole garlic clove added
to a dish will give it the
flavor but not the pungency
of garlic; a halved clove will
add a little "bite"; a finely
chopped garlic clove will
release most of its flavor;
and a crushed clove will
release all of the flavor.

1 Heat the oil in a medium-size
pan. Add the onion slices and
cook until golden brown, stirring.

2 Add the red chilies, half the
chopped cilantro, and the
tomatoes to the pan, then reduce the
heat to a simmer.

3 Add the salt, ginger, garlic, and
chili powder to the mixture in the
pan and stir well.

4 Add the ground lamb to the
pan and stir-fry the mixture for
7–10 minutes.

5 Add the peas to the mixture in the
pan and cook for an additional
3–4 minutes, stirring occasionally.

6 Transfer to serving plates and
garnish with green chilies and the
remaining cilantro.

NUTRITION	
Calories 357	Sugars 3g
Protein 25g	Fat 26g
Carbohydrate 6g	Saturates 6g

moroccan lamb kabobs

serves four

1 lb/450 g lean lamb

1 lemon

1 red onion

4 small zucchini

couscous, to serve (see Cook's Tip)

MARINADE

grated rind and juice of 1 lemon

2 tbsp olive oil

1 garlic clove, crushed

1 fresh red chili, sliced (optional)

1 tsp ground cinnamon

1 tsp ground ginger

½ tsp ground cumin

½ tsp ground coriander

COOK'S TIP

Serve these kabobs with couscous. Allowing ⅓ cup couscous per person, soak the couscous in cold water for 20 minutes, or until softened. Drain and steam for 10 minutes, or until piping hot.

1 Cut the lamb into even, bite-size chunks and place in a large nonmetallic dish.

2 To make the marinade, mix the lemon rind and juice, oil, garlic, chili, if using, cinnamon, ginger, cumin, and coriander together.

3 Pour the marinade over the lamb and toss to coat. Cover and let marinate in the refrigerator for at least 2 hours, or preferably overnight.

4 Preheat the grill. Cut the lemon into 8 pieces. Cut the onion into wedges, then separate each wedge into 2 pieces.

5 Using a canelle knife or potato peeler, cut thin strips of peel from the zucchini, then cut the zucchini into even-size chunks.

6 Remove the meat from the marinade, reserving the liquid for basting. Thread the meat onto metal skewers, alternating with the onion, lemon, and zucchini.

7 Cook over hot coals for 8–10 minutes, turning and basting with the marinade. Serve on a bed of couscous (see Cook's Tip).

NUTRITION	
Calories 348	Sugars 2g
Protein 30g	Fat 24g
Carbohydrate 2g	Saturates 10g

lamb with bay & lemon

serves four

4 lamb chops

1 tbsp corn oil

1 tbsp butter

⅔ cup white wine

⅔ cup lamb or vegetable stock

2 bay leaves

pared rind of 1 lemon

salt and pepper

NUTRITION

Calories 268	Sugars 0.2g
Protein 24g	Fat 16g
Carbohydrate 0.2g	Saturates 7g

COOK'S TIP

Your local butcher will offer you good advice on how to prepare the lamb noisettes, if you are wary of preparing them yourself.

1 Using a sharp knife, carefully remove the bone from each lamb chop, keeping the meat intact. Alternatively, ask the butcher to prepare the lamb noisettes for you.

2 Shape the meat into rounds and secure with a length of string.

3 Heat the oil and butter together in a large skillet until the mixture begins to froth.

4 Add the lamb noisettes to the skillet and cook for 2–3 minutes on each side, or until browned all over.

5 Remove the pan from the heat. Remove the meat, then drain off all of the excess fat and discard. Place the noisettes back in the pan.

6 Return the pan to the heat. Add the wine, stock, bay leaves, and lemon rind and cook for 20–25 minutes, or until the lamb is tender. Season the lamb and sauce to taste with a little salt and pepper.

7 Transfer to serving plates. Remove the string from each noisette and serve with the sauce.

red wine lamb skewers

serves four

1 lb/450 g lean lamb

12 pearl onions or shallots, unpeeled

12 white mushrooms

MARINADE

⅔ cup red wine

4 tbsp olive oil

2 tbsp brandy (optional)

1 onion, sliced

1 bay leaf

fresh thyme sprig

2 fresh parsley sprigs

TO SERVE

salad greens

cherry tomatoes

1 Carefully trim away any excess fat from the lamb. Cut the lamb into large pieces.

2 To make the marinade, mix the wine, oil, brandy, if using, onion, bay leaf, thyme, and parsley together in a nonmetallic dish.

NUTRITION

Calories 353	Sugars 5g
Protein 24g	Fat 21g
Carbohydrate 7g	Saturates 6g

3 Add the meat and toss to coat. Cover and let marinate in the refrigerator for at least 2 hours, or preferably overnight.

4 Preheat the grill. Bring a pan of water to a rolling boil, then drop in the pearl onions and blanch them for 3 minutes. Drain and refresh under cold water, and then drain again. Trim the onions and remove their skins.

5 Remove the meat from the marinade, reserving the liquid for basting. Thread the meat onto metal skewers, alternating with the pearl onions and mushrooms.

6 Cook the kabobs over hot coals for 8–10 minutes, turning and basting the meat and vegetables with the reserved marinade a few times.

7 Transfer the kabobs to warmed serving plates and serve with salad greens and cherry tomatoes.

lamb chops with rosemary

serves four

8 lamb chops

5 tbsp olive oil

2 tbsp lemon juice

1 garlic clove, crushed

½ tsp lemon pepper

salt

8 fresh rosemary sprigs

SALAD

4 tomatoes, sliced

4 scallions, diagonally sliced

DRESSING

2 tbsp olive oil

1 tbsp lemon juice

1 garlic clove, chopped

¼ tsp finely chopped fresh
  rosemary

NUTRITION	
Calories 560	Sugars 1g
Protein 48g	Fat 40g
Carbohydrate 1g	Saturates 13g

1 Preheat the grill. Trim the lamb by cutting away the flesh to expose the tips of the bones.

2 Place the oil, lemon juice, garlic, lemon pepper, and salt in a shallow nonmetallic dish and whisk with a fork to combine.

3 Lay the rosemary in the dish and place the lamb on top. Cover and let marinate in the refrigerator for at least 1 hour, turning once.

4 Remove the chops from the marinade and wrap foil around the exposed bones to stop them from burning.

5 Place the rosemary sprigs on the rack and place the lamb on top. Cook over hot coals for 10–15 minutes, turning once.

6 Meanwhile, make the salad and dressing. Arrange the tomatoes on a serving dish and sprinkle the scallions on top. Place all the ingredients for the dressing in a screw-top jar, then shake well and pour over the salad. Serve with the grilled lamb chops.

lamb with olives

serves four

2 lb 12 oz/1.25 kg boned leg
  of lamb

6 tbsp olive oil

2 garlic cloves, crushed

1 onion, sliced

1 small fresh red chili, seeded and
  finely chopped

¾ cup dry white wine

1 cup pitted black olives

salt

1 fresh flatleaf parsley sprig,
  to garnish

NUTRITION

Calories 577	Sugars 1g
Protein 62g	Fat 33g
Carbohydrate 1g	Saturates 10g

1 Preheat the oven to 350°F/180°C. Cut the lamb into 1-inch/2.5-cm cubes with a sharp knife.

2 Heat the oil in a skillet over medium heat. Add the garlic, onion, and chili and cook for 5 minutes.

3 Add the meat and wine and cook for an additional 5 minutes.

4 Stir in the olives, then transfer the mixture to a casserole. Cook in the preheated oven for 1 hour 20 minutes, or until the meat is tender. Season to taste with salt. Transfer to a serving plate, then garnish with a parsley sprig and serve.

lamb & anchovies with thyme

serves four

1 tbsp corn oil

1 tbsp butter

1 lb 5 oz/600 g boneless lamb
(shoulder or leg), cut into 1-inch/
2.5-cm chunks

4 garlic cloves, peeled

3 fresh thyme sprigs, stems removed

6 canned anchovy fillets, drained

⅔ cup red wine

⅔ cup lamb or vegetable stock

1 tsp sugar

scant ⅓ cup black olives, pitted
and halved

2 tbsp chopped fresh parsley,
to garnish

NUTRITION

Calories 577	Sugars 1g
Protein 62g	Fat 33g
Carbohydrate 1g	Saturates 10g

COOK'S TIP

This dish is excellent served with
Charbroiled Vegetables
(see page 189).

1 Heat the oil and butter in a large skillet. Add the lamb and cook for 4–5 minutes, stirring, until the meat is browned all over.

2 Using a pestle and mortar, grind the garlic, thyme, and anchovies together to make a smooth paste.

3 Add the wine and stock to the skillet. Stir in the garlic and anchovy paste together with the sugar.

4 Bring the mixture to a boil, then reduce the heat and let simmer, covered, for 30–40 minutes, or until the lamb is tender. For the last 10 minutes of the cooking time, remove the lid in order to let the sauce reduce slightly.

5 Stir the olives into the sauce and mix to combine.

6 Transfer the lamb and its sauce to a serving bowl and garnish with chopped parsley. Serve.

pork stir-fry with vegetables

serves four

2 tbsp vegetable oil

2 garlic cloves, crushed

½-inch/1-cm piece fresh gingerroot, cut into slivers

12 oz/350 g lean pork tenderloin, thinly sliced

1 carrot, cut into thin strips

1 red bell pepper, seeded and diced

1 fennel bulb, sliced

1 oz/25 g canned water chestnuts, drained and halved

1½ cups fresh bean sprouts

2 tbsp rice wine

1¼ cups pork or chicken stock

pinch of brown sugar

1 tsp cornstarch

2 tsp water

1 Heat the oil in a preheated wok. Add the garlic, ginger, and pork. Stir-fry for 1–2 minutes, or until the meat is sealed.

2 Add the carrot, bell pepper, fennel, and water chestnuts and stir-fry for 2–3 minutes.

NUTRITION

Calories 216	Sugars 3g
Protein 19g	Fat 12g
Carbohydrate 5g	Saturates 3g

3 Add the bean sprouts and stir-fry for 1 minute. Remove the pork and vegetables and keep warm.

4 Add the rice wine, stock, and sugar to the wok. Blend the cornstarch to a smooth paste with the water and stir it into the sauce. Bring to a boil, stirring constantly, and cook until thickened and clear.

5 Return the meat and vegetables to the wok and cook for 1–2 minutes, or until heated through and coated with the sauce. Serve immediately.

VARIATION

Use dry sherry instead of the rice wine if you have difficulty obtaining it.

baked ham with sauce

serves four–six

4 lb 8 oz–6 lb 8 oz/2–3 kg whole
 boneless cured ham

2 bay leaves

1–2 onions, cut into fourths

2 carrots, thickly sliced

6 cloves

GLAZE

1 tbsp red currant jelly

1 tbsp whole-grain mustard

CUMBERLAND SAUCE

1 orange

3 tbsp red currant jelly

2 tbsp lemon or lime juice

2 tbsp orange juice

2–4 tbsp port

1 tbsp whole-grain mustard

TO GARNISH

salad greens

orange slices

NUTRITION

Calories 414	Sugars 4g
Protein 70g	Fat 13g
Carbohydrate 4g	Saturates 5g

1 Place the ham in a large pan. Add the bay leaves, onions, carrots, and cloves and cover with cold water. Bring to a boil over low heat, then cover and simmer for half the cooking time. To calculate the cooking time, allow 30 minutes per 1 lb 2 oz/500 g plus 30 minutes.

2 Preheat the oven to 350°F/180°C. Drain the meat and remove the skin. Place the meat in a roasting pan and score the fat. To make the glaze, combine the ingredients and spread over the fat. Cook in the oven for the remainder of the cooking time. Baste at least once.

3 To make the sauce, pare the rind from half the orange and cut into strips. Cook in boiling water for 3 minutes. Drain.

4 Place all the remaining sauce ingredients in a small pan and heat gently, stirring occasionally, until the red currant jelly dissolves. Add the orange rind strips and simmer gently for an additional 3–4 minutes.

5 Slice the ham and place on a warmed serving platter. Garnish with salad greens and orange slices and serve with the Cumberland sauce.

griddled pork with orange sauce

serves four

4 tbsp freshly squeezed orange juice

4 tbsp red wine vinegar

2 garlic cloves, finely chopped

pepper

4 pork steaks, trimmed of all
   visible fat

olive oil, for brushing

GREMOLATA

3 tbsp finely chopped fresh parsley

grated rind of 1 lime

grated rind of ½ lemon

1 garlic clove, very finely chopped

NUTRITION

Calories 204	Sugars 1g
Protein 26g	Fat 10g
Carbohydrate 2g	Saturates 3g

1 Mix the orange juice, vinegar, and garlic together in a shallow, nonmetallic dish and season to taste with pepper. Add the pork, turning to coat. Cover and let marinate in the refrigerator for up to 3 hours.

2 Meanwhile, mix all the Gremolata ingredients together in a small mixing bowl, then cover with plastic wrap and let chill in the refrigerator until required.

3 Heat a nonstick grill pan and brush lightly with olive oil. Remove the pork from the marinade, reserving the marinade, and add to the pan. Cook over medium–high heat for 5 minutes on each side, or until the juices run clear when the meat is pierced with the tip of a sharp knife.

4 Meanwhile, pour the marinade into a small pan and let simmer over medium heat for 5 minutes, or until slightly thickened. Transfer the pork to a serving dish, then pour the orange sauce over it and sprinkle with the Gremolata. Serve immediately.

VARIATION

This dish would work equally well with chicken breast portions. Remove the skin from the cooked chicken before serving.

stuffed pork with prosciutto

serves four

1 lb 2 oz/500 g piece pork
   tenderloin, trimmed of excess fat

salt and pepper

small bunch of fresh basil
   leaves, washed

2 tbsp freshly grated Parmesan
   cheese

2 tbsp sun-dried tomato paste

6 thin slices prosciutto

1 tbsp olive oil

salad greens, to serve

OLIVE PASTE

⅓ cup pitted black olives

2 garlic cloves, peeled

4 tbsp olive oil

COOK'S TIP

Choose a good lean piece of pork
tenderloin for the best results.

NUTRITION

Calories 427	Sugars 0g
Protein 31g	Fat 34g
Carbohydrate 0.2g	Saturates 7g

1 Preheat the oven to 375°F/190°C. Slice the pork lengthwise down the center, taking care not to cut all the way through. Open out the pork and season the inside with salt and pepper.

2 Lay the basil leaves down the center of the pork. Mix the cheese and sun-dried tomato paste together and spread over the basil.

3 Press the pork back together. Wrap the prosciutto around the pork, overlapping, to cover. Place on a rack in a roasting pan, seam-side down, and brush with oil. Bake in the preheated oven for 30–40 minutes, depending on thickness, until cooked through. Let stand for 10 minutes.

4 To make the olive paste, place all the ingredients in a food processor and process until smooth. Alternatively, for a coarser paste, finely chop the olives and garlic and mix with the oil.

5 Drain the cooked pork and slice. Serve with the olive paste and salad greens.

pork & sage kabobs

serves twelve

1 lb/450 g ground lean pork

2 tbsp fresh bread crumbs

1 small onion, very finely chopped

1 tbsp chopped fresh sage

2 tbsp applesauce

¼ tsp ground nutmeg

salt and pepper

BASTE

3 tbsp olive oil

1 tbsp lemon juice

TO SERVE

6 tbsp thick plain yogurt

mixed salad greens

NUTRITION

Calories 96	Sugars 0g
Protein 8g	Fat 7g
Carbohydrate 2g	Saturates 2g

1 Place the ground pork in a large bowl. Add the bread crumbs, onion, sage, applesauce, and nutmeg, then season to taste with salt and pepper, and mix until well combined.

2 Using your hands, shape the mixture into balls, about the size of large marbles. Cover and let chill in the refrigerator for at least 30 minutes.

3 Preheat the grill. Soak 12 small wooden skewers in cold water for 30 minutes. Thread the meatballs onto the skewers.

4 To make the baste, mix the oil and lemon juice in a small bowl, whisking with a fork until blended.

5 Cook the kabobs over hot coals, turning and basting, for 8–10 minutes, or until the meat is cooked through.

6 Spoon some of the yogurt over the salad greens. Serve immediately with the grilled pork kabobs.

carnitas

serves four–six

2 lb 4 oz/1 kg pork, such as
   lean belly

1 onion, chopped

1 garlic bulb, cut in half

½ tsp ground cumin

2 meat stock cubes

2 bay leaves

salt and pepper

fresh chili strips, to garnish

salsa of your choice,
   to serve

NUTRITION

Calories 236		Sugars 1g	
Protein 36g		Fat 9g	
Carbohydrate 3g		Saturates 3g	

1 Place the pork in a heavy-bottom skillet with the onion, garlic, cumin, stock cubes, and bay leaves. Add just enough water to cover. Bring to a boil, then reduce the heat to very low. Skim off the foam and scum that forms on the surface.

2 Simmer very gently for 2 hours, or until the meat is cooked through and tender. Remove the skillet from the heat and let the meat cool in the cooking liquid.

3 Remove the meat from the skillet with a slotted spoon. Cut off any rind (roast separately to make cracklings). Cut the meat into bite-size pieces and season to taste with salt and pepper. Reserve 1¼ cups of the cooking liquid.

4 Brown the meat in a heavy-bottom skillet for 15 minutes to cook out the fat. Add the reserved cooking liquid and reduce. Cover and cook for an additional 15 minutes, turning the meat occasionally.

5 Transfer the meat to a serving dish and garnish with chili strips. Serve with salsa.

pork with daikon

serves four

4 tbsp vegetable oil

1 lb/450 g lean pork tenderloin

1 eggplant

8 oz/225 g daikon

2 garlic cloves, crushed

3 tbsp light soy sauce

2 tbsp sweet chili sauce

NUTRITION

Calories 280	Sugars 1g
Protein 25g	Fat 19g
Carbohydrate 2g	Saturates 4g

COOK'S TIP

Daikon are long white vegetables common in Chinese cooking. Usually grated, they have a milder flavor than red radish. They are generally available in most large supermarkets.

1 Heat 2 tablespoons of the oil in a preheated wok or large heavy-bottom skillet.

2 Using a sharp knife, thinly slice the pork into even-size pieces.

3 Add the slices of pork to the wok and stir-fry for 5 minutes.

4 Using a sharp knife, trim and dice the eggplant. Peel and thinly slice the daikon.

5 Add the remaining vegetable oil to the wok.

6 Add the diced eggplant to the wok together with the garlic and stir-fry for 5 minutes.

7 Add the daikon to the wok and stir-fry for 2 minutes.

8 Stir the soy sauce and sweet chili sauce into the mixture in the wok and cook until heated through.

9 Transfer the pork to serving bowls and serve immediately.

ham steaks with apple rings

serves four

4 ham steaks, about 6 oz/
175 g each

1–2 tsp whole-grain mustard

1 tbsp clear honey

2 tbsp lemon juice

1 tbsp corn oil

APPLE RINGS

2 green dessert apples

2 tsp raw brown sugar

¼ tsp ground nutmeg

¼ tsp ground cinnamon

¼ tsp ground allspice

1–2 tbsp melted butter

NUTRITION	
Calories 358	Sugars 13g
Protein 31g	Fat 21g
Carbohydrate 13g	Saturates 8g

1 Preheat the grill. Using a pair of scissors, make a few cuts around the edges of the ham steaks to prevent them curling up as they cook. Spread a little whole-grain mustard over the steaks.

2 Mix the honey, lemon juice, and oil together in a bowl.

3 To prepare the apple rings, core the apples and cut them into thick slices. Mix the sugar with the spices and press the apple slices in the mixture until well coated on both sides.

4 Cook the ham steaks over hot coals for 3–4 minutes on each side, basting frequently with the honey and lemon mixture.

COOK'S TIP

Ham can be a little salty. If you have time, soak the steaks in cold water for 30–60 minutes before cooking—this process will remove the excess salt.

5 Meanwhile, brush the apple slices with melted butter and cook them over the hot coals, alongside the ham steaks, for 3–4 minutes, turning once and brushing with melted butter as they cook.

6 Serve the ham steaks with the cooked apple slices.

thai stir-fried chicken

serves four

3 tbsp sesame oil

12 oz/350 g skinless, boneless
   chicken breast, thinly sliced

salt and pepper

8 shallots, sliced

2 garlic cloves, finely chopped

2 tsp grated fresh gingerroot

1 fresh green chili, seeded and
   finely chopped

1 red bell pepper, seeded and
   thinly sliced

1 green bell pepper, seeded and
   thinly sliced

3 zucchini, thinly sliced

2 tbsp ground almonds

1 tsp ground cinnamon

1 tbsp oyster sauce

¾ oz/20 g creamed coconut, grated

1 Heat the oil in a preheated wok
   or heavy-bottom skillet. Add the
chicken and season to taste with salt
and pepper, then stir-fry over medium
heat for 4 minutes.

2 Add the shallots, garlic, ginger,
   and chili and stir-fry for an
additional 2 minutes.

NUTRITION	
Calories 184	Sugars 6g
Protein 24g	Fat 5g
Carbohydrate 8g	Saturates 2g

3 Add the red and green bell
   peppers and zucchini and stir-fry
for 1 minute.

4 Stir in the almonds, cinnamon,
   oyster sauce, and creamed
coconut and season to taste with salt
and pepper. Stir-fry for 1 minute to
heat through, then serve immediately.

COOK'S TIP
Creamed coconut is sold in
supermarkets and Asian stores.
It is a useful pantry standby
because it adds richness and
depth of flavor.

sweet mango chicken

serves four

1 tbsp corn oil

6 skinless, boneless chicken thighs

1 ripe mango

2 garlic cloves, crushed

8 oz/225 g leeks, shredded

1¾ cups bean sprouts

⅔ cup mango juice

1 tbsp white wine vinegar

2 tbsp clear honey

2 tbsp tomato ketchup

1 tsp cornstarch

NUTRITION

Calories 244	Sugars 18g
Protein 27g	Fat 7g
Carbohydrate 2.1g	Saturates 2g

COOK'S TIP

Mango juice is available in jars from most supermarkets and is quite thick and sweet. If it is unavailable, purée and strain a ripe mango and add a little water to make up the required quantity.

1 Heat the oil in a preheated wok or large skillet.

2 Cut the chicken into bite-size cubes. Add to the wok and stir-fry over high heat for 10 minutes, tossing frequently until the chicken is cooked through and golden in color.

3 Peel, pit, and slice the mango and add to the wok with the garlic, leeks, and bean sprouts. Stir-fry for an additional 2–3 minutes, or until softened.

4 Mix the mango juice, vinegar, honey, ketchup, and cornstarch together. Pour into the wok and stir-fry for an additional 2 minutes, or until the juices begin to thicken.

5 Transfer to a warmed serving plate and serve immediately.

karahi chicken

serves four

2 tbsp ghee

3 garlic cloves, crushed

1 onion, finely chopped

2 tbsp garam masala

1 tsp coriander seeds, ground

½ tsp dried mint

1 bay leaf

1 lb 10 oz/750 g lean boneless
   chicken, diced

generous ¾ cup chicken stock

1 tbsp chopped cilantro

salt

mixed salad, to serve

NUTRITION

Calories 270	Sugars 1g
Protein 41g	Fat 11g
Carbohydrate 1g	Saturates 2g

1 Heat the ghee in a preheated karahi, wok, or large heavy-bottom skillet. Add the garlic and onion and stir-fry for 4 minutes, or until the onion is golden.

2 Stir in the garam masala, coriander, mint, and bay leaf.

3 Add the diced chicken and cook over high heat, stirring occasionally, for 5 minutes. Add the stock, then reduce the heat and simmer for 10 minutes, or until the sauce has thickened and the chicken is thoroughly cooked and tender.

4 Stir in the cilantro and season to taste with salt, then mix well. Serve immediately with a mixed salad.

COOK'S TIP

It is important always to heat a karahi or wok before you add the oil to help maintain the high temperature.

minty lime chicken

serves six

3 tbsp finely chopped fresh mint

4 tbsp clear honey

4 tbsp lime juice

12 boneless chicken thighs

SAUCE

⅔ cup thick plain yogurt

1 tbsp finely chopped fresh mint

2 tsp finely grated lime rind

mixed salad, to serve

COOK'S TIP

Mint can be grown very easily in a garden or window box. It is a useful herb for marinades and salad dressings. Other useful herbs to grow are parsley and basil.

1 Mix the mint, honey, and lime juice together in a bowl.

2 Use wooden toothpicks to keep the chicken thighs in neat shapes and place in a large nonmetallic bowl. Add the marinade to the chicken and turn to coat evenly.

VARIATION

Use this marinade for chicken kabobs, alternating the chicken with lime and red onion wedges.

3 Cover and let marinate in the refrigerator for at least 30 minutes, or preferably overnight. Preheat the grill or broiler to medium. Cook the chicken over the hot coals or under the hot broiler, turning frequently and basting with the marinade, until the chicken is tender and the juices run clear when a skewer or tip of a knife is inserted into the thickest part of the meat.

4 Meanwhile, mix all the ingredients for the sauce together in a bowl. Remove the toothpicks from the chicken and serve immediately with the sauce and a mixed salad.

NUTRITION

Calories 170	Sugars 12g
Protein 23g	Fat 3g
Carbohydrate 12g	Saturates 1g

chicken & ginger stir-fry

serves four

3 tbsp corn oil

1 lb 9 oz/700 g lean skinless,
boneless chicken breasts, cut into
2-inch/5-cm strips

3 garlic cloves, crushed

1½-inch/4-cm piece fresh
gingerroot, cut into strips

1 tsp pomegranate seeds,
crushed

½ tsp ground turmeric

1 tsp garam masala

2 fresh green chilies, sliced

½ tsp salt

4 tbsp lemon juice

grated rind of 1 lemon

6 tbsp chopped cilantro

½ cup chicken stock

COOK'S TIP

Stir-frying is perfect for lowfat diets, because only a little oil is needed. Cooking the food over high heat ensures that food is sealed and cooked quickly to hold in the flavor.

1 Heat the oil in a preheated wok or large skillet. Add the chicken and stir-fry until golden brown all over. Remove from the wok and reserve.

2 Add the garlic, ginger, and pomegranate seeds to the wok and cook in the oil for 1 minute, taking care not to let the garlic burn.

3 Stir in the turmeric, garam masala, and chilies and cook for 30 seconds.

4 Return the chicken to the wok and add the salt, lemon juice and rind, cilantro, and stock. Stir the chicken well to make sure it is coated in the sauce.

5 Bring the mixture to a boil, then reduce the heat and simmer for 10–15 minutes, or until the chicken is cooked and tender. Serve.

NUTRITION	
Calories 291	Sugars 0g
Protein 41g	Fat 14g
Carbohydrate 0g	Saturates 3g

135

chicken in banana leaves

serves four–six

1 garlic clove, chopped

1 tsp finely chopped fresh
gingerroot

¼ tsp pepper

2 cilantro sprigs

1 tbsp Thai fish sauce

1 tbsp whiskey

3 skinless, boneless chicken breasts

2–3 banana leaves, cut into 3-inch/
7.5-cm squares

corn oil, for pan-frying

chili dipping sauce, to serve

NUTRITION

Calories 185	Sugars 0g
Protein 18g	Fat 12g
Carbohydrate 0.5g	Saturates 1g

1 Place the garlic, ginger, pepper, cilantro, fish sauce, and whiskey in a mortar and, using a pestle, grind to a smooth paste.

2 Cut the chicken into 1-inch/ 2.5-cm chunks and toss in the paste to coat. Cover and let marinate in the refrigerator for 1 hour.

3 Place a piece of chicken on a square of banana leaf and wrap it up like a package to enclose the chicken completely. Secure with wooden toothpicks or tie with string.

4 Heat a ⅛–inch/3–mm depth of oil in a large heavy-bottom skillet until hot.

5 Pan-fry the packages for 8–10 minutes, turning them over occasionally, until golden brown and the chicken is thoroughly cooked. Serve with a chili dipping sauce.

COOK'S TIP

To make a sweet chili dipping sauce to serve with the chicken pieces, mix together equal amounts of chili sauce and tomato ketchup, then stir in a dash of rice wine to taste.

green salsa chicken breasts

serves four

4 skinless chicken breast fillets

salt and pepper

all-purpose flour, for dusting

2–3 tbsp butter or a mixture of
butter and vegetable oil

2⅓ cups mild green salsa or
puréed tomatillos

1 cup chicken stock

1–2 garlic cloves, finely chopped

3–5 tbsp chopped cilantro

½ fresh green chili, seeded
and chopped

½ tsp ground cumin

TO SERVE

1 cup sour cream

romaine lettuce leaves, shredded

3–5 scallions, thinly sliced

coarsely chopped cilantro

1 Sprinkle the chicken with salt and pepper to taste, then dredge in flour. Shake off the excess.

2 Melt the butter or heat the butter and oil mixture in a large heavy-bottom skillet. Add the chicken and cook over medium–high heat, turning once, until the fillets are golden all over but not quite cooked through—they will continue to cook slightly in the sauce. Remove from the pan and reserve.

NUTRITION

Calories 349		Sugars 7g
Protein 34g		Fat 20g
Carbohydrate 10g		Saturates 12g

3 Place the salsa, stock, garlic, cilantro, chili, and cumin in a pan and bring to a boil. Reduce the heat to a low simmer. Add the chicken breasts to the sauce, spooning the sauce over the chicken. Continue to cook until the chicken is cooked through and tender.

4 Remove the chicken from the pan and season to taste with salt and pepper. Serve immediately with the sour cream, shredded lettuce, sliced scallions, and chopped cilantro.

chicken with balsamic vinegar

serves four

4 boneless chicken thighs

2 garlic cloves, crushed

generous ¾ cup red wine

3 tbsp white wine vinegar

salt and pepper

1 tbsp corn oil

1 tbsp butter

4 shallots

3 tbsp balsamic vinegar

2 tbsp chopped fresh thyme

NUTRITION

Calories 148	Sugars 0.2g
Protein 11g	Fat 8g
Carbohydrate 0.2g	Saturates 3g

1 Using a sharp knife, make a few slashes in the skin of the chicken. Brush the chicken with the crushed garlic and place in a nonmetallic dish.

2 Pour the wine and wine vinegar over the chicken and season to taste with salt and pepper. Cover with plastic wrap and let marinate in the refrigerator overnight.

COOK'S TIP

To make the chicken pieces look a little neater, use wooden skewers to hold them together or secure them with a length of string.

3 Remove the chicken pieces with a slotted spoon, draining well, and reserve the marinade.

4 Heat the oil and butter in a skillet. Add the shallots and cook, stirring, for 2–3 minutes, or until they begin to soften.

5 Add the chicken pieces to the skillet and cook for 3–4 minutes, turning, until browned all over. Reduce the heat and add half the reserved marinade. Cover and cook for 15–20 minutes, adding more marinade when necessary.

6 Once the chicken is tender, add the balsamic vinegar and thyme and cook for an additional 4 minutes.

7 Transfer the chicken and marinade to serving plates and serve.

chicken in spicy yogurt

serves four

3 dried red chilies

2 tbsp coriander seeds

2 tsp ground turmeric

2 tsp garam masala

4 garlic cloves, crushed

½ onion, chopped

1-inch/2.5-cm piece fresh
   gingerroot, grated

2 tbsp lime juice

1 tsp salt

½ cup lowfat plain yogurt

1 tbsp corn oil

4 lb 8 oz/2 kg skinless chicken,
   cut into 6 pieces, or
   6 chicken portions

fresh mint sprigs, to garnish

TO SERVE

chopped tomatoes

diced cucumber

sliced red onion

raita

NUTRITION

Calories 74	Sugars 2g
Protein 9g	Fat 4g
Carbohydrate 2g	Saturates 1g

1 Grind the chilies, coriander seeds, turmeric, garam masala, garlic, onion, ginger, lime juice, and salt together in a mortar using a pestle.

2 Gently heat a skillet and add the spice mixture. Stir-fry for 2 minutes, or until fragrant, then turn into a shallow nonmetallic dish.

3 Add the yogurt and oil to the spice paste and mix well.

4 Make 3 slashes in the flesh of each piece of chicken. Add to the yogurt and spice mixture and coat the pieces in the marinade. Cover and chill in the refrigerator for at least 4 hours. Remove from the refrigerator and let stand, covered, at room temperature for 30 minutes before cooking.

5 Preheat the grill. Wrap the chicken pieces in foil, sealing well so the juices cannot escape.

6 Cook the chicken over very hot coals for 15 minutes, turning once. Remove the foil and cook for an additional 5 minutes.

7 Garnish the chicken with mint sprigs and serve with tomatoes, cucumber, onion, and raita.

141

jerk chicken

serves four

4 lean chicken portions

1 bunch of scallions

1–2 fresh habanero
    chilies, seeded

1 garlic clove

2-inch/5-cm piece fresh gingerroot,
    coarsely chopped

½ tsp dried thyme

½ tsp paprika

¼ tsp ground allspice

pinch of ground cinnamon

pinch of ground cloves

4 tbsp white wine vinegar

3 tbsp light soy sauce

pepper

1 Place the chicken portions in a shallow nonmetallic dish.

2 Place the scallions, chilies, garlic, ginger, thyme, paprika, allspice, cinnamon, cloves, vinegar, soy sauce, and pepper to taste in a food processor and process until smooth.

3 Pour the spicy mixture over the chicken. Turn the chicken portions over so that they are well coated in the marinade.

4 Transfer the chicken portions to the refrigerator and let marinate for up to 24 hours.

5 Preheat the grill. Remove the chicken from the marinade and cook over medium–hot coals for 30 minutes, turning the chicken over and basting occasionally with any remaining marinade, until the chicken is browned and cooked through.

6 Transfer the chicken portions to individual serving plates and serve immediately.

NUTRITION	
Calories 158	Sugars 0.4g
Protein 29g	Fat 4g
Carbohydrate 2g	Saturates 1g

lemongrass skewers

serves four

2 long or 4 short lemongrass stems

2 large skinless, boneless chicken
  breasts, coarsely chopped

1 small egg white

1 carrot, finely grated

1 small fresh red chili, seeded and
  chopped

2 tbsp chopped fresh garlic chives

2 tbsp chopped cilantro

salt and pepper

1 tbsp corn oil

TO GARNISH

cilantro sprigs

lime slices

NUTRITION

Calories 140	Sugars 2g
Protein 19g	Fat 7g
Carbohydrate 2g	Saturates 1g

COOK'S TIP

If you can't find lemongrass
stems, use wooden or bamboo
skewers instead and add
½ teaspoon ground lemongrass
with the other flavorings.

1 If the lemongrass stems are long, cut them in half across the center to make 4 short lengths. Cut each stalk in half lengthwise, so you have 8 lemongrass stems altogether.

2 Place the chicken pieces in a food processor with the egg white. Process to a smooth paste, then add the carrot, chili, garlic chives, cilantro, and salt and pepper to taste. Process for a few seconds to mix well.

3 Cover and let the mixture chill in the refrigerator for 15 minutes. Preheat the broiler to medium. Divide the mixture into 8 equal-size portions and use your hands to shape the mixture around the lemongrass "skewers."

4 Brush the skewers with oil and cook under the hot broiler, turning them occasionally, for 4–6 minutes, or until golden brown and thoroughly cooked. Alternatively, grill over medium–hot coals.

5 Garnish with cilantro sprigs and lime slices and serve hot.

citrus duckling skewers

serves twelve

3 skinless, boneless duckling breasts

1 small red onion, cut into wedges

1 small eggplant, cut into cubes

MARINADE

grated rind and juice of 1 lemon

grated rind and juice of 1 lime

grated rind and juice of 1 orange

1 garlic clove, crushed

1 tsp dried oregano

2 tbsp olive oil, plus extra for oiling

dash of Tabasco sauce

COOK'S TIP

For more zing, add 1 teaspoon of chili sauce to the marinade. The meat can be marinated for several hours, but it is best to marinate the vegetables separately for only 30 minutes.

1 Cut the duckling into bite-size pieces. Place in a nonmetallic bowl with the prepared vegetables.

2 To make the marinade, place the lemon, lime, and orange rinds and juices, garlic, oregano, oil, and Tabasco in a screw-top jar and shake until well combined. Pour the marinade over the duckling and vegetables and toss to coat. Cover and let marinate in the refrigerator for 30 minutes.

3 Preheat the grill. Remove the duck and vegetables from the marinade and thread them onto presoaked wooden skewers, reserving the marinade.

4 Cook the skewers on an oiled rack over medium–hot coals, turning and basting frequently with the reserved marinade, for 15–20 minutes, or until the meat is cooked through. Alternatively, cook under a preheated broiler. Serve immediately.

NUTRITION	
Calories 205	Sugars 5g
Protein 24g	Fat 10g
Carbohydrate 5g	Saturates 2g

duck with berry sauce

serves four

1 lb/450 g boneless duck breasts

2 tbsp raspberry vinegar

2 tbsp brandy

1 tbsp clear honey

salt and pepper

1 tsp corn oil, for brushing

SAUCE

generous 1½ cups raspberries,
    thawed if frozen

1¼ cups rosé wine

2 tsp cornstarch blended with
    4 tsp cold water

TO SERVE

2 kiwifruit, peeled and thinly sliced

assorted vegetables

1 Skin and trim the duck breasts to remove any excess fat. Using a sharp knife, score the flesh in diagonal lines. Pound with a meat mallet or rolling pin until ¾ inch/2 cm thick.

2 Place the duck breasts in a shallow nonmetallic dish. Mix the vinegar, brandy, and honey together in a small bowl and spoon it over the duck. Cover and let chill in the refrigerator for 1 hour.

3 Preheat the broiler. Drain the duck breasts, reserving the marinade, and place on the broiler rack. Season to taste with salt and pepper and brush with a little oil. Cook for 10 minutes under the hot broiler and turn over, then season and brush with oil again. Cook for an additional 8–10 minutes, or until the meat is cooked through.

NUTRITION

Calories 293	Sugars 10g
Protein 28g	Fat 8g
Carbohydrate 13g	Saturates 2g

4 Meanwhile, make the sauce. Reserve about ⅓ cup raspberries and place the rest in a pan. Add the reserved marinade and the wine. Bring to a boil, then reduce the heat and simmer for 5 minutes, or until slightly reduced. Strain the sauce into a bowl, pressing the raspberries with the back of a spoon. Return the liquid to the pan and add the cornstarch paste. Heat through, stirring, until thickened. Add the reserved raspberries and season to taste with salt and pepper.

5 Thinly slice the duck breasts and alternate with slices of kiwifruit. on warmed serving plates. Spoon over the sauce and serve with vegetables.

turkey stuffed with cheese

serves four

4 turkey breast pieces, about
  8 oz/225 g each

salt and pepper

4 portions soft cheese, such as
  Bel Paese, ½ oz/15 g each

4 fresh sage leaves or
  ½ tsp dried sage

8 lean bacon slices

4 tbsp olive oil

2 tbsp lemon juice

TO SERVE

salad greens

cherry tomatoes

NUTRITION

Calories 518	Sugars 0g
Protein 66g	Fat 28g
Carbohydrate 0g	Saturates 9g

VARIATION

You can vary the cheese you use
to stuff the turkey—try grated
mozzarella or slices of Brie or
Camembert. Also try 1 teaspoon
of red currant jelly or cranberry
sauce in each slit instead
of the sage.

1 Preheat the grill. Carefully cut a slit into the side of each turkey breast. Open out each breast a little and season inside to taste with salt and pepper.

2 Place a portion of cheese in each slit. Tuck a sage leaf into each slit or sprinkle with a little dried sage.

3 Stretch each bacon slice with the back of a knife. Wrap 2 pieces around each turkey breast, covering the slit.

4 Mix the oil and lemon juice together in a small bowl.

5 Cook the turkey over medium–hot coals, basting frequently with the oil and lemon mixture, for 10 minutes on each side, or until cooked through and tender.

6 Transfer the turkey to warmed serving plates. Serve with salad greens and cherry tomatoes.

Fish & Seafood

This selection of recipes exploits the contrasting characteristics of different fish and shellfish to the full. Fish that come in handy single-portion size are cooked whole for maximum succulence as well as ease of preparation, either with sealed-in seasonings in foil packages, such as Lemon Herrings (see page 150), or directly on the grill rack in the case of Mediterranean Sardines (see page 156). The firm texture of tuna, swordfish, and halibut, on the other hand, makes them ideally suited to the speedy searing of steaks in a ridged grill pan. Shrimp are also given the fast-food treatment, either stir-fried in Garlic Shrimp (see page 172) or deep-fried after initial marinating for enhanced flavor in Spicy Salt & Pepper Shrimp (see page 169).

Lively, exotic flavorings abound in this chapter, from Mussels with Lemongrass (see page 173) to Indonesian-Style Spicy Cod (see page 179).

lemon herrings

serves four

4 herrings, cleaned and scaled

4 bay leaves

salt

1 lemon, sliced

4 tbsp unsalted butter

2 tbsp chopped fresh parsley

½ tsp lemon pepper

NUTRITION

Calories 355	Sugars 0g
Protein 19g	Fat 31g
Carbohydrate 0g	Saturates 13g

1 Preheat the grill. Season the prepared herrings inside and out to taste with salt.

2 Place a bay leaf inside the cavity of each fish.

3 Place 4 squares of foil on the counter and divide the lemon slices evenly between them. Place a fish on top of the lemon slices on each of the foil squares.

4 Beat the butter until softened in a bowl, then mix in the parsley and lemon pepper. Dot the flavored butter liberally all over the fish.

5 Wrap the fish tightly in the foil and cook over medium–hot coals for 15–20 minutes, or until the fish is cooked through—the flesh should be white in color and firm to the touch (unwrap the foil to check if the fish is cooked, then rewrap).

6 Transfer the wrapped fish packages to warmed serving plates.

7 Open the foil packages just before serving, but serve the fish in their cooking juices still in the packages.

3

4

5

blackened fish

serves four

4 white fish steaks

1 tbsp paprika

1 tsp dried thyme

1 tsp cayenne pepper

1 tsp black pepper

½ tsp white pepper

½ tsp salt

¼ tsp ground allspice

3½ tbsp unsalted butter

3 tbsp corn oil

mixed salad greens, to serve

NUTRITION

Calories 331	Sugars 0g
Protein 37g	Fat 20g
Carbohydrate 0g	Saturates 8g

COOK'S TIP

A whole fish—red snapper, for example—rather than steaks is also delicious cooked this way. The spicy seasoning can also be used to coat chicken portions, if you prefer.

1 Preheat the grill. Rinse the fish under cold running water and pat dry with paper towels.

2 Mix the paprika, thyme, cayenne, black and white peppers, salt, and allspice together in a shallow dish.

3 Place the butter and oil in a small pan and heat over low heat, stirring occasionally, until the butter has melted.

4 Brush the butter mixture liberally all over the fish steaks on both sides.

5 Dip the fish into the spicy mix until well coated on both sides.

6 Cook the fish over hot coals for 10 minutes on each side, turning once. Continue to baste the fish with the remaining butter mixture during the cooking time. Transfer the fish to 4 large serving plates and serve with mixed salad greens.

butterfly shrimp

serves two–four

1 lb 2 oz/500 g or 16 raw jumbo
    shrimp, shelled and tails
    left intact

juice of 2 limes

1 tsp cardamom seeds

2 tsp cumin seeds, ground

2 tsp coriander seeds, ground

½ tsp ground cinnamon

1 tsp ground turmeric

1 garlic clove, crushed

1 tsp cayenne pepper

2 tbsp corn oil

cucumber slices, to garnish

NUTRITION

Calories 183	Sugars 0g
Protein 28g	Fat 8g
Carbohydrate 0g	Saturates 1g

1 Soak 8 wooden skewers in a bowl of water for 20 minutes. Cut the shells lengthwise in half down to the tail and flatten out to form a symmetrical shape.

2 Thread a shrimp onto 2 presoaked wooden skewers, with the tail between them, so that, when laid flat, the skewers hold the shrimp in shape. Thread another 3 shrimp onto these 2 skewers in the same way.

3 Repeat until you have 4 sets of 4 shrimp each.

4 Lay the skewered shrimp in a nonmetallic dish and sprinkle over the lime juice.

5 Mix the spices and oil together, then coat the shrimp well in the mixture. Cover the shrimp and let chill in the refrigerator for 4 hours.

6 Preheat the grill or broiler. Cook over hot coals or place in a broiler pan lined with foil and cook under the hot broiler for 6 minutes, turning once.

7 Serve immediately, garnished with cucumber slices.

mackerel with lime & cilantro

serves four

4 small mackerel, cleaned and scaled

¼ tsp ground coriander

¼ tsp ground cumin

salt and pepper

3 tbsp chopped cilantro

1 fresh red chili, seeded and
    chopped

grated rind and juice of 1 lime

2 tbsp corn oil

TO GARNISH

fresh red chili flowers
    (see Cook's Tip—optional)

1 lime, sliced

salad greens, to serve

NUTRITION

Calories 302	Sugars 0g
Protein 21g	Fat 24g
Carbohydrate 0g	Saturates 4g

1 Preheat the grill. Make the chili flowers for the garnish (see Cook's Tip). Remove the heads from the prepared mackerel. Sprinkle the mackerel with the spices and season to taste with salt and pepper. Sprinkle 1 teaspoon of the cilantro inside the cavity of each fish.

2 Mix the remaining cilantro, chili, lime rind and juice, and oil together in a small bowl. Brush the mixture liberally over the fish.

3 Cook the fish cook over hot coals for 3–4 minutes on each side, turning once. Brush frequently with the basting mixture. Transfer the fish to serving plates and garnish with chili flowers, if using, and lime slices. Serve with salad greens.

COOK'S TIP

To make the chili flowers, cut the tip of 8 small chilies lengthwise into thin strips, leaving the chilies intact at the stem end. Remove the seeds and place the chilies in ice water until curled.

marinated fish

serves four

4 whole mackerel

4 tbsp chopped fresh marjoram

2 tbsp extra virgin olive oil

finely grated rind and juice of 1 lime

2 garlic cloves, crushed

salt and pepper

lime wedges, to garnish

salad greens, to serve

NUTRITION	
Calories 361	Sugars 0g
Protein 26g	Fat 29g
Carbohydrate 0g	Saturates 5g

1 Using a sharp knife, clean and scale the fish (see page 156), then cut 4–5 diagonal slashes on each side of the fish. Place the fish in a shallow nonmetallic dish.

2 To make the marinade, mix the marjoram, oil, lime rind and juice, garlic, and salt and pepper to taste together in a bowl.

3 Pour the mixture over the fish. Cover and let marinate in the refrigerator for 30 minutes.

4 Preheat the broiler, then cook the mackerel under the hot broiler for 5–6 minutes on each side, brushing occasionally with the reserved marinade, until golden.

5 Transfer the fish to serving plates. Pour over any remaining marinade, then garnish with lime wedges and serve with salad greens.

mediterranean sardines

serves four

8–12 whole fresh sardines

8–12 fresh thyme sprigs

salt and pepper

3 tbsp lemon juice

4 tbsp olive oil

TO GARNISH

lemon wedges

tomato slices

mixed salad

NUTRITION

Calories 857	Sugars 0g
Protein 88g	Fat 56g
Carbohydrate 0g	Saturates 11g

VARIATION

For a slightly different flavor and texture, give the sardines a crispy coating by tossing them in dried bread crumbs and basting them with a little olive oil.

1 Preheat the grill. Clean the fish if this has not already been done.

2 Remove the scales from the sardines by rubbing the back of a knife from tail to head along the body. Wash the sardines and pat dry with paper towels.

3 Tuck a thyme sprig into the body cavity of each sardine.

4 Transfer the sardines to a large nonmetallic dish and season to taste with salt and pepper.

5 Beat the lemon juice and oil together in a bowl and pour the mixture over the sardines. Cover and let marinate in the refrigerator for 30 minutes.

6 Remove the sardines from the marinade and place them in a hinged basket, if you have one, or on a rack. Cook the sardines over hot coals for 3–4 minutes on each side, basting frequently with any remaining marinade.

7 Serve the cooked sardines garnished with lemon wedges, tomato slices, and a mixed salad.

tuna with anchovy butter

serves four

4 thick tuna steaks, about 8 oz/
225 g each and ¾ inch/2 cm thick

olive oil, for oiling

ANCHOVY BUTTER

8 anchovy fillets in oil, drained

4 scallions, finely chopped

1 tbsp finely grated orange rind

1 stick unsalted butter

¼ tsp lemon juice

salt and pepper

TO GARNISH

fresh flatleaf parsley sprigs

orange rind strips

NUTRITION

Calories 564	Sugars 0g
Protein 55g	Fat 38g
Carbohydrate 0g	Saturates 19g

VARIATION

If you like your food particularly
hot and spicy, add a pinch of
dried chili flakes to the anchovy
butter mixture for a little
extra punch.

1 Preheat the grill. To make the anchovy butter, very finely chop the anchovies and place them in a bowl with the scallions, orange rind, and softened butter. Beat until all the ingredients are blended well together, seasoning to taste with lemon juice and pepper.

2 Place the flavored butter on a sheet of parchment paper and roll up into a log shape. Fold over the ends and place in the freezer for 15 minutes to become firm.

3 Cook the tuna steaks for 2 minutes on an oiled grill rack over hot coals. Alternatively, cook in an oiled, ridged grill pan over high heat, in batches if necessary. Turn the steaks over and cook for 2 minutes for rare or up to 4 minutes for well done. Season to taste with salt and pepper.

4 Transfer the tuna steaks to warmed serving plates and place 2 thin slices of anchovy butter on each steak. Garnish with parsley sprigs and strips of orange rind and serve.

skate with black butter

serves four

2 lb/900 g skate wings, cut into 4

1½ sticks butter

4 tbsp red wine vinegar

½ oz/15 g capers, drained

1 tbsp chopped fresh parsley

salt and pepper

COURT-BOUILLON

3½ cups cold water

3½ cups dry white wine

3 tbsp white wine vinegar

2 large carrots, coarsely chopped

1 onion, coarsely chopped

2 celery stalks, coarsely chopped

2 leeks, coarsely chopped

2 garlic cloves, coarsely chopped

2 bay leaves

4 fresh parsley sprigs

4 fresh thyme sprigs

6 black peppercorns

1 tsp salt

green vegetables, to serve

NUTRITION

Calories 381	Sugars 0g
Protein 34g	Fat 27g
Carbohydrate 0g	Saturates 17g

1 Begin by making the court-bouillon. Place all the ingredients in a large pan and bring slowly to a boil. Reduce the heat, then cover and simmer gently for 30 minutes. Strain the liquid through a fine strainer into a clean pan. Return to a boil, then simmer fast, uncovered, for 15–20 minutes, or until reduced to 2½ cups.

2 Place the skate in a wide shallow pan and pour the court-bouillon over it. Bring to a boil, then reduce the heat and simmer very gently for 15 minutes or a little longer, depending on the thickness of the skate. Drain the fish and put to one side, keeping it warm.

3 Meanwhile, melt the butter in a skillet. Cook over medium heat until the butter changes color to a dark brown and smells very nutty.

4 Add the vinegar, capers, and parsley and simmer for 1 minute. Season to taste with salt and pepper. Pour over the fish. Serve with seasonal fresh green vegetables of your choice.

smoky fish skewers

serves four

12 oz/350 g smoked cod fillet

12 oz/350 g cod fillet

8 large raw shrimp

8 bay leaves

fresh dill sprigs, to garnish (optional)

MARINADE

4 tbsp corn oil, plus extra
    for oiling

2 tbsp lemon or lime juice

grated rind of ½ lemon or lime

¼ tsp dried dill

salt and pepper

NUTRITION

Calories 221	Sugars 0g
Protein 33g	Fat 10g
Carbohydrate 0g	Saturates 1g

1 Skin both types of cod and cut the flesh into bite-size pieces. Shell the shrimp, leaving the tails intact.

2 To make the marinade, mix the oil, lemon juice and rind, dried dill, and salt and pepper to taste together in a shallow nonmetallic dish.

3 Place the prepared fish in the marinade and stir well until the fish is coated on all sides. Cover and let marinate in the refrigerator for 30 minutes.

4 Preheat the grill. Thread the seafood onto 4 metal skewers, alternating the fish with the shrimp and bay leaves.

COOK'S TIP

Cod fillet can be rather flaky, so choose the thicker end, which is easier to cut into chunky pieces. Cook the fish on foil rather than directly on the rack, so that if the fish breaks away from the skewer it is not wasted.

5 Cover the grill rack with lightly oiled foil. Place the fish skewers on top and cook over hot coals for 5–10 minutes, basting with any remaining marinade. Turn once.

6 Transfer the skewers to a warmed serving plate and garnish with dill sprigs, if using, then serve.

stuffed angler fish tail

1 lb 10 oz/750 g angler fish tail,
   skinned and trimmed

6 slices prosciutto

4 tbsp chopped fresh mixed herbs,
   such as parsley, chives, basil,
   and sage

1 tsp finely grated lemon rind

salt and pepper

2 tbsp olive oil

shredded stir-fried vegetables,
   to serve

NUTRITION

Calories 154		Sugars 0g
Protein 24g		Fat 6g
Carbohydrate 0g		Saturates 1g

1 Preheat the oven to 400°F/200°C. Using a sharp knife, carefully cut down each side of the central bone of the angler fish to leave 2 fillets. Rinse the fillets under cold running water and pat dry with paper towels.

2 Lay the prosciutto slices widthwise on a counter so that they overlap slightly. Lay the fish fillets lengthwise on top of the ham so that the 2 cut sides face each other.

3 Mix the chopped herbs and lemon rind together. Season well with salt and pepper. Pack this mixture onto the cut surface of 1 angler fish fillet. Press the 2 fillets together and wrap tightly with the prosciutto slices. Secure with string or wooden toothpicks.

4 Heat the oil in a large skillet over low heat. Place the fish in the pan, seam-side down first, and brown the wrapped fish all over.

5 Transfer the fish to a large ovenproof dish and cook in the preheated oven for 25 minutes, or until golden and the fish is tender. Remove from the oven and let rest for 10 minutes before slicing thickly. Serve with shredded stir-fried vegetables.

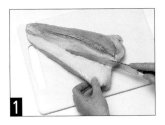

szechuan white fish

serves four

1 small egg, beaten

3 tbsp all-purpose flour

4 tbsp dry white wine

3 tbsp light soy sauce

12 oz/350 g white fish fillets, cut
into 1½-inch/4-cm cubes

vegetable oil, for frying

1 garlic clove, cut into slivers

1 tsp finely chopped fresh
gingerroot

1 onion, finely chopped

1 celery stalk, chopped

1 fresh red chili, chopped

3 scallions, chopped

1 tsp rice wine vinegar

½ tsp ground Szechuan pepper

¾ cup fish stock

1 tsp superfine sugar

1 tsp cornstarch

2 tsp water

NUTRITION

Calories 225	Sugars 3g	
Protein 20g	Fat 8g	
Carbohydrate 17g	Saturates 1g	

1 Beat the egg, flour, wine, and 1 tablespoon of the soy sauce together in a bowl to make a batter. Dip the fish into the batter to coat well.

2 Heat the oil in a preheated wok or large heavy-bottom skillet. Reduce the heat slightly, then add the fish in batches and cook for 2–3 minutes, or until golden brown. Remove the fish with a slotted spoon and drain on paper towels. Keep warm.

3 Pour all but 1 tablespoon of the oil from the wok and return it to the heat. Add the garlic, ginger, onion, celery, chili, and scallions and stir-fry for 1–2 minutes. Stir in the remaining soy sauce and the vinegar.

4 Add the Szechuan pepper, stock, and sugar to the wok. Mix the cornstarch with the water to form a smooth paste and stir it into the stock. Bring to a boil and cook, stirring, for 1 minute, or until the sauce thickens and clears.

5 Return the fish to the wok and cook for 1–2 minutes. Serve immediately.

thai-spiced salmon

serves four

1-inch/2.5-cm piece fresh
  gingerroot, grated

1 tsp coriander seeds,
  crushed

½ tsp chili powder

1 tbsp lime juice

1 tsp sesame oil

4 pieces salmon fillet with skin,
  about 5½ oz/150 g each

2 tbsp vegetable oil

stir-fried vegetables, to serve

NUTRITION

Calories 329	Sugars 0.1g	
Protein 30g	Fat 23g	
Carbohydrate 0.1g	Saturates 4g	

COOK'S TIP

Use a heavy-bottom skillet or grill pan so that the fish cooks evenly throughout without sticking. If it is very thick, turn it over carefully to cook on the other side for 2–3 minutes.

1 Mix the ginger, crushed coriander, chili powder, lime juice, and sesame oil together.

2 Place the salmon on a wide nonmetallic plate or dish and spoon the mixture over the flesh side of the fillets, spreading it to coat each piece of salmon evenly.

3 Cover the dish and chill in the refrigerator for 30 minutes.

4 Heat a wide heavy-bottom skillet or grill pan with the vegetable oil over high heat. Place the salmon in the hot pan, skin-side down.

5 Cook the salmon for 4–5 minutes, without turning, until the salmon is crusty underneath and the flesh flakes easily. Serve immediately with stir-fried vegetables.

baked sea bass

serves four

2 sea bass, about 2 lb 4 oz/1 kg
each, cleaned and scaled

2 scallions, green part only,
cut into strips

2-inch/5-cm piece fresh gingerroot,
cut into strips

2 garlic cloves, unpeeled and
lightly crushed

2 tbsp mirin or dry sherry

salt and pepper

TO SERVE

pickled sushi ginger (optional)

soy sauce

NUTRITION

Calories 140	Sugars 0.1g
Protein 29g	Fat 1g
Carbohydrate 0.1g	Saturates 0.2g

1 Preheat the grill. For each fish, lay out a double thickness of foil and oil the top piece well or lay a piece of parchment paper over the foil.

2 Place the fish in the center of the foil and expose the cavities. Divide the scallions, ginger, and garlic between each cavity.

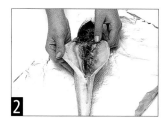

3 Pour the mirin over the fish and season to taste with salt and pepper.

4 Close the cavities and lay each fish on its side. Fold over the foil to encase the fish and seal the edges securely. Fold each end neatly.

5 Cook over medium–hot coals for 15 minutes, turning once.

6 To serve, remove the foil and cut each fish into 2–3 pieces. Serve with the pickled sushi ginger, if using, accompanied by soy sauce.

COOK'S TIP

Fresh sea bass is just as delicious when cooked very simply. Stuff the fish with garlic and chopped herbs and brush with olive oil, then bake in the oven.

salmon fillet with herbs

serves four

½ large bunch of dried thyme

5 fresh rosemary branches,
  6–8 inches/15–20 cm long

8 bay leaves

2 lb 4 oz/1 kg salmon fillet

1 fennel bulb, cut into 8 pieces

2 tbsp lemon juice

2 tbsp olive oil

fresh salad greens, to serve

NUTRITION

Calories 507	Sugars 0.4g	
Protein 46g	Fat 35g	
Carbohydrate 0.5g	Saturates 6g	

1 Preheat the grill. Make a base on the hot grill with the thyme, rosemary, and bay leaves, overlapping them so that they cover a slightly larger area than the salmon.

2 Carefully place the salmon on top of the herbs.

VARIATION

Use whatever combination of herbs you may have to hand—but avoid the stronger tasting herbs, such as sage and marjoram, which are unsuitable for fish.

3 Arrange the fennel around the edge of the fish.

4 Mix the lemon juice and oil together, then brush the salmon with it. Cover the salmon loosely with a piece of foil, to keep it moist.

5 Cook over hot coals for 20–30 minutes, basting frequently with the lemon mixture.

6 Remove the cooked salmon from the grill and cut it into slices, then arrange the fennel around it. Serve with salad greens.

noisettes of salmon

serves four

4 salmon steaks

3½ tbsp butter, softened

1 garlic clove, crushed

2 tsp mustard seeds

2 tbsp chopped fresh thyme

1 tbsp chopped fresh parsley

salt and pepper

2 tbsp vegetable oil

4 tomatoes, peeled, seeded,
    and chopped

green vegetables or salad,
    to serve

NUTRITION

Calories 381	Sugars 3g	
Protein 36g	Fat 26g	
Carbohydrate 3g	Saturates 4g	

COOK'S TIP

You can make cod steaks into
noisettes in the same way. Cook
them with butter flavored with
fresh chives and basil.

1 Preheat the oven to 400°F/200°C. Carefully remove the central bone from the salmon steaks and cut them in half. Curl each piece around to form a noisette and tie with string. Blend the butter, garlic, mustard seeds, thyme, parsley, and salt and pepper to taste together in a bowl and reserve.

2 Heat the oil in a preheated ridged grill pan or large skillet over medium heat. Add the salmon noisettes and brown on both sides, in batches if necessary. Drain on paper towels and let cool.

3 Cut 4 pieces of parchment paper into 12-inch/30-cm squares. Place 2 salmon noisettes on top of each square and top with a little of the flavored butter and chopped tomato. Draw up the edges of the paper and fold together to enclose the fish. Place on a cookie sheet.

4 Cook in the preheated oven for 10–15 minutes, or until the salmon is cooked through. Serve while still warm with green vegetables or salad of your choice.

spicy salt & pepper shrimp

serves four

9–10½ oz/250–300 g raw shrimp
in shells, thawed if frozen

1 tbsp light soy sauce

1 tsp rice wine or dry sherry

2 tsp cornstarch

vegetable oil, for deep-frying

2–3 scallions, to garnish

SPICY SALT & PEPPER

1 tbsp salt

1 tsp ground Szechuan peppercorns

1 tsp Chinese five-spice powder

NUTRITION

Calories 160	Sugars 0.2g
Protein 17g	Fat 10g
Carbohydrate 0.5g	Saturates 1g

1 Pull the soft legs off the shrimp, but keep the body shell on. Dry well on paper towels.

2 Place the shrimp in a bowl with the soy sauce, rice wine, and cornstarch. Turn the shrimp to coat thoroughly in the mixture, then cover and let marinate in the refrigerator for 25–30 minutes.

3 To make the Spicy Salt & Pepper, mix the salt, ground Szechuan peppercorns, and five-spice powder together in a bowl. Place in a dry skillet and stir-fry for 3–4 minutes over low heat, stirring constantly to prevent the spices burning on the bottom of the skillet. Remove from the heat and let cool.

4 Heat the oil in a preheated wok or large skillet until smoking. Add the shrimp, in batches, and deep-fry until golden brown. Remove the shrimp from the wok with a slotted spoon and drain on paper towels.

5 Place the scallions in a bowl, pour over 1 tablespoon of the hot oil, and let stand for 30 seconds. Serve the shrimp garnished with the scallions, with the Spicy Salt & Pepper as a dip.

fish with yucatan flavors

serves eight

4 tbsp annatto seeds, soaked in
   water overnight

3 garlic cloves, finely chopped

1 tbsp mild chili powder

1 tbsp paprika

1 tsp ground cumin

½ tsp dried oregano

2 tbsp beer or tequila

juice of 1 lime and 1 orange or
   3 tbsp pineapple juice

2 tbsp olive oil

2 tbsp chopped cilantro

¼ tsp ground cinnamon

¼ tsp ground cloves

2 lb 4 oz/1 kg swordfish steaks

banana leaves, for wrapping
   (optional)

cilantro sprigs, to garnish

orange wedges, to serve

NUTRITION

Calories 179		Sugars 1g	
Protein 24g		Fat 8g	
Carbohydrate 1g		Saturates 2g	

1 Drain the annatto, then crush them to a paste in a mortar using a pestle. Work in the garlic, chili powder, paprika, cumin, oregano, beer, fruit juice, oil, cilantro, cinnamon, and cloves.

2 Smear the paste over the fish, then cover and let marinate in the refrigerator for at least 3 hours or overnight.

3 Preheat the grill or broiler. Wrap the fish steaks in banana leaves, tying with string to make packages. Bring enough water to a boil in a steamer, then add a batch of packages to the top part of the steamer and steam for 15 minutes, or until the fish is cooked through.

4 Alternatively, cook the fish without wrapping in the banana leaves. To cook on the grill, place in a hinged basket or on a rack and cook over hot coals for 5–6 minutes on each side, or until cooked through. Alternatively, cook the fish under the hot broiler for 5–6 minutes on each side, or until cooked through.

5 Garnish with cilantro sprigs and serve with orange wedges for squeezing over the fish.

garlic shrimp

serves four

½ cup olive oil

4 garlic cloves, finely chopped

2 hot fresh red chilies, seeded and
    finely chopped

1 lb/450 g cooked jumbo shrimp

2 tbsp chopped fresh
    flatleaf parsley

salt and pepper

lemon wedges, to garnish

NUTRITION

Calories 385	Sugars 0g
Protein 26g	Fat 31g
Carbohydrate 1g	Saturates 5g

COOK'S TIP

If you can get hold of raw
shrimp, cook them as above but
increase the cooking time to
5–6 minutes, or until the shrimp
are cooked through and turn
bright pink. If you are using
frozen shrimp, make sure they
are thoroughly thawed
before cooking.

1 Heat the oil in a large heavy-bottom skillet over low heat. Add the garlic and chilies and cook, stirring occasionally, for 1–2 minutes, or until softened but not colored.

2 Add the shrimp and stir-fry for 2–3 minutes, or until heated through and coated in the oil and garlic mixture.

3 Turn off the heat and add the chopped parsley, stirring well to mix. Season to taste with salt and pepper.

4 Divide the shrimp and garlic-flavored oil between warmed serving dishes. Garnish with lemon wedges and serve.

mussels with lemongrass

serves four

1 lb 10 oz/750 g live mussels

1 tbsp sesame oil

3 shallots, finely chopped

2 garlic cloves, finely chopped

1 lemongrass stem

2 fresh kaffir lime leaves

2 tbsp chopped cilantro

finely grated rind of 1 lime

2 tbsp lime juice

1¼ cups hot vegetable stock

cilantro, to garnish

NUTRITION

Calories 194	Sugars 0g
Protein 33g	Fat 7g
Carbohydrate 1g	Saturates 1g

COOK'S TIP

Mussels are now farmed, so they should be available throughout the year.

1 Clean the mussels thoroughly by scrubbing or scraping the shells and pulling out any beards that are attached to them. Discard any with broken shells or any that refuse to close when tapped.

2 Heat the oil in a large pan. Add the shallots and garlic and cook gently for 2 minutes, or until softened.

3 Bruise the lemongrass, using a meat mallet or rolling pin, and add to the pan with the lime leaves, cilantro, lime rind and juice, mussels, and stock. Cook, covered, over high heat for 3–4 minutes, shaking the pan occasionally, until the mussels have opened.

4 Lift the mussels out into 4 warmed soup plates, discarding any that remain closed. Boil the remaining liquid rapidly to reduce slightly. Remove and discard the lemongrass and lime leaves, then pour the liquid over the mussels. Garnish with cilantro and serve.

thai steamed mussels

serves two

2 lb 4 oz/1 kg live mussels

2 shallots, finely chopped

1 lemongrass stem, finely sliced

1 garlic clove, finely chopped

3 tbsp rice wine or dry sherry

2 tbsp lime juice

1 tbsp Thai fish sauce

4 tbsp chopped fresh basil

salt and pepper

2 tbsp butter

fresh basil leaves, to garnish

NUTRITION

Calories 252	Sugars 2g
Protein 22g	Fat 14g
Carbohydrate 8g	Saturates 8g

COOK'S TIP

If you prefer to serve this dish as an appetizer, this amount will be enough for 4 portions. Fresh clams in shells are also very good when cooked by this method.

1 Clean the mussels thoroughly by scrubbing or scraping the shells and pulling out any beards that are attached to them. Discard any with broken shells or any that refuse to close when tapped.

2 Place the shallots, lemongrass, garlic, rice wine, lime juice, and fish sauce in a large heavy-bottom pan and place over high heat.

3 Add the mussels, then cover and cook for 3–4 minutes, shaking the pan occasionally, until the mussels have opened.

4 Discard any mussels that remain closed, then stir in the chopped basil and season to taste with salt and pepper.

5 Scoop out the mussels with a slotted spoon and divide between 2 deep bowls. Quickly whisk the butter into the pan juices, then pour the juices over the mussels.

6 Garnish each bowl with basil leaves and serve.

red curry fish cakes

serves six

2 lb 4 oz/1 kg fish fillets or prepared
   seafood, such as cod, haddock,
   shrimp, crabmeat, or lobster
1 egg, beaten
2 tbsp chopped cilantro
6 tbsp Thai red curry paste
1 bunch of scallions,
   finely chopped
vegetable oil, for deep-frying
fresh red chili flowers, to garnish
   (see page 154)
CUCUMBER SALAD
1 large cucumber, peeled
   and grated
2 shallots, grated
2 fresh red chilies, seeded and very
   finely chopped
2 tbsp Thai fish sauce
2 tbsp dried powdered shrimp
1½–2 tbsp lime juice

NUTRITION

Calories 203	Sugars 1g
Protein 32g	Fat 8g
Carbohydrate 1g	Saturates 1g

1 Place the fish in a food processor
   with the egg, cilantro, and curry
paste and process until smooth and
well blended.

2 Transfer the mixture to a bowl,
   then add the scallions and mix
well to combine.

3 Taking 2 tablespoons of the fish
   mixture at a time, shape into
balls, then flatten them slightly with
your fingers to make fish cakes.

4 Heat the oil in a preheated wok
   or skillet until hot.

5 Add a few fish cakes to the wok
   and deep-fry for a few minutes
until brown and cooked. Remove and
drain on paper towels. Keep warm
while cooking the remaining fish cakes.

6 To make the salad, mix the
   cucumber, shallots, chilies, fish
sauce, dried shrimp, and lime juice
together. Garnish the salad with a chili
flower and serve with the fish cakes.

gingered angler fish

NUTRITION

Calories 133	Sugars 0g
Protein 21g	Fat 5g
Carbohydrate 1g	Saturates 1g

1 Cut the angler fish into bite-size pieces. Mix the ginger and sweet chili sauce together in a small bowl until thoroughly blended. Brush the ginger and chili sauce mixture over the fish pieces using a pastry brush.

2 Heat the corn oil in a preheated wok or large heavy-bottom skillet.

3 Add the fish, asparagus, and scallions to the wok and stir-fry for 5 minutes, stirring gently so the fish and asparagus do not break up.

4 Remove the wok from the heat. Drizzle the sesame oil over the stir-fry and toss well to combine.

5 Transfer the fish mixture to warmed serving plates and serve immediately.

COOK'S TIP

Angler fish is quite expensive, but it is well worth using, because it has a wonderful flavor and texture. You could use cubes of chunky cod fillet instead.

swordfish steaks

4 swordfish steaks, about
   5½ oz/150 g each

4 tbsp olive oil

1 garlic clove, crushed

1 tsp lemon rind

parsley sprigs, to garnish

SALSA VERDE

scant ½ cup fresh flatleaf parsley

¼ cup mixed fresh herbs, such as
   basil, mint, and chives

1 garlic clove, chopped

1 tbsp capers, drained and rinsed

1 tbsp green peppercorns in
   brine, drained

4 canned anchovy fillets in oil,
   drained and coarsely chopped

1 tsp Dijon mustard

½ cup extra virgin olive oil

salt and pepper

NUTRITION

Calories 548	Sugars 0g
Protein 28g	Fat 48g
Carbohydrate 1g	Saturates 7g

1 Rinse the swordfish steaks under cold running water and pat dry with paper towels. Arrange the steaks in a nonmetallic dish. Mix the oil, garlic, and lemon rind together in a small bowl and pour over the swordfish steaks. Cover and let marinate in the refrigerator for 1 hour.

2 To make the Salsa Verde, place the parsley, mixed herbs, garlic, capers, green peppercorns, anchovies, mustard, and oil in a food processor and process to a smooth paste, adding a little warm water if necessary. Season to taste with salt and pepper and reserve.

3 Remove the swordfish steaks from the marinade. Transfer to a preheated ridged grill pan and cook for 2–3 minutes on each side, or until tender. Transfer the fish to 4 large serving plates and garnish with parsley sprigs, then serve immediately with the Salsa Verde.

COOK'S TIP

Firm-fleshed fish is ideal for this recipe. Try tuna or shark instead.

indonesian-style spicy cod

serves four

4 cod steaks

1 lemongrass stem

1 small red onion, chopped

3 garlic cloves, chopped

2 fresh red chilies, seeded
  and chopped

1 tsp grated fresh gingerroot

¼ tsp ground turmeric

salt and pepper

2 tbsp butter, cut into small cubes

8 tbsp canned coconut milk

2 tbsp lemon juice

fresh red chilies, to garnish
  (optional)

mixed salad greens, to serve

NUTRITION

Calories 146	Sugars 2g
Protein 19g	Fat 7g
Carbohydrate 2g	Saturates 4g

COOK'S TIP

If you prefer a milder flavor, omit
the chilies altogether. For a hotter
flavor, do not remove the seeds
from the chilies.

1 Preheat the grill. Rinse the cod steaks under cold running water and pat dry on paper towels.

2 Remove and discard the outer leaves from the lemongrass and thinly slice the inner section.

3 Place the lemongrass, onion, garlic, chilies, ginger, and turmeric in a food processor and process until finely chopped. Season to taste with salt and pepper. With the motor running, add the butter, coconut milk, and lemon juice and process until well blended.

4 Place the fish in a shallow nonmetallic dish. Pour over the coconut mixture and turn the fish until well coated.

5 If you have one, place the fish steaks in a hinged basket, which will make them easier to turn. Cook the fish steaks over hot coals for 15 minutes, or until the fish is cooked through, turning once. Transfer to 4 large serving plates and garnish with red chilies, if using, then serve with mixed salad greens.

pan-seared halibut

1 tsp olive oil

4 halibut steaks, skinned, about
   6 oz/175 g each

½ tsp cornstarch mixed with 2 tsp
   cold water

2 tbsp snipped fresh chives,
   to garnish

RED ONION RELISH

2 red onions

6 shallots

1 tbsp lemon juice

2 tsp olive oil

2 tbsp red wine vinegar

2 tsp superfine sugar

⅔ cup fish stock

salt and pepper

COOK'S TIP

If raw onions make your eyes
water, try peeling them under
cold running water. Alternatively,
stand or sit well back from the
onion so that your face isn't
directly over it.

1 To make the relish, shred the
onions and shallots thinly, then
place in a small bowl and toss in the
lemon juice.

2 Heat the oil for the relish in a
skillet over medium heat. Add the
onions and shallots and cook for
3–4 minutes, or until just softened.

3 Add the vinegar and sugar and
cook for an additional 2 minutes
over high heat. Pour in the stock and
season well with salt and pepper. Bring
to a boil, then reduce the heat and
simmer gently for an additional
8–9 minutes, or until the sauce has
thickened and is slightly reduced.

4 Brush a nonstick ridged grill pan
or skillet with oil and heat over
medium–high heat until hot. Press
the fish steaks into the pan to seal,
then reduce the heat and cook for
4 minutes. Turn the fish over and cook
for 4–5 minutes, or until cooked
through. Drain the fish on paper towels
and keep warm.

5 Stir the cornstarch paste into the
onion relish and heat through,
stirring, until thickened. Season to taste
with salt and pepper.

6 Pile the relish onto 4 warmed
serving plates and place a fish
steak on top of each. Garnish with
snipped chives and serve.

NUTRITION

Calories 197	Sugars 1g
Protein 31g	Fat 7g
Carbohydrate 2g	Saturates 1g

trout in red wine

serves four

4 fresh trout, about 10½ oz/
   300 g each

generous 1 cup red or white
   wine vinegar

1¼ cups red or dry
   white wine

⅔ cup water

1 carrot, sliced

2–4 bay leaves

thinly pared rind of 1 lemon

1 small onion, very thinly sliced

4 fresh parsley sprigs

4 fresh thyme sprigs

1 tsp black peppercorns

6–8 whole cloves

salt and pepper

¾ stick butter

TO GARNISH

fresh parsley sprigs

lemon slices

mixed salad, to serve

NUTRITION

Calories 489	Sugars 0.6g
Protein 48g	Fat 27g
Carbohydrate 0.6g	Saturates 14g

1 Clean the trout but leave their heads on. Dry on paper towels and lay the fish head to tail in a shallow container or baking pan large enough to hold them.

2 Bring the vinegar to a boil and pour slowly all over the fish. Cover and let the fish marinate in the refrigerator for 20 minutes.

3 Meanwhile, place the wine, water, carrot, bay leaves, lemon rind, onion, herbs, peppercorns, and cloves in a pan with a good pinch of salt and heat gently.

4 Drain the fish thoroughly, discarding the vinegar. Place the fish in a fish kettle or large skillet so they touch. When the wine mixture boils, strain gently over the fish so they are about half covered. Cover and simmer very gently for 15 minutes.

5 Carefully remove the fish from the kettle, draining off and reserving as much of the liquid as possible. Arrange the fish in a serving dish and keep warm.

6 Boil the cooking liquid until reduced to 4–6 tablespoons. Melt the butter in a pan and strain in the cooking liquor. Season and spoon over the fish. Garnish with parsley and lemon slices and serve with salad.

Vegetables

Vegetables are too good to be confined to a supporting role in your diet, especially in a low-carbohydrate eating plan. So here they take center stage in a range of imaginative, flavorful dishes. Enjoy the colorful medley of bell peppers, zucchini, and baby eggplants, threaded onto skewers, in the recipe for Charbroiled Vegetables (see page 189), or savor the aromatic spices in the rich red Tomato Curry (see page 204).

In other recipes in this chapter, you will find vegetables perfectly partnered with a choice protein, such as vegetarian smoked tofu in Marinated Brochettes (see page 186) and fluffy eggs in Spinach & Herb Frittata (see page 211). You can even enjoy your vegetables with a limited amount of carbohydrates, with tender asparagus encased in crisp phyllo pastry and juicy mushrooms stuffed with a creamy potato filling.

marinated brochettes

serves four

1 lemon

1 garlic clove, crushed

4 tbsp olive oil

4 tbsp white wine vinegar

1 tbsp chopped fresh herbs, such as
    rosemary, parsley, and thyme

salt and pepper

10½ oz/300 g smoked tofu, drained

12 oz/350 g mushrooms

fresh herbs, to garnish

TO SERVE

mixed salad greens

cherry tomatoes

NUTRITION

Calories 192	Sugars 0.5g
Protein 11g	Fat 16g
Carbohydrate 1g	Saturates 2g

1 Finely grate the rind from the lemon and squeeze out the juice into a bowl.

2 Add the garlic, oil, vinegar, and chopped herbs and mix well. Season to taste with salt and pepper.

3 Slice the tofu into large chunks with a sharp knife. Thread the pieces onto presoaked wooden skewers, alternating them with the mushrooms.

4 Place the brochettes in a shallow nonmetallic dish and pour over the marinade. Cover and let chill in the refrigerator for 1–2 hours, turning in the marinade occasionally.

5 Preheat the grill or broiler. Remove the brochettes from the dish, reserving the marinade. Cook over medium–hot coals, brushing them frequently with the marinade and turning often, for 6 minutes, or until cooked through and golden brown. Alternatively, cook under the hot broiler, turning frequently and brushing with the reserved marinade.

6 Transfer to warmed serving plates and garnish with fresh herbs. Serve immediately with mixed salad greens and cherry tomatoes.

braised tofu home-style

serves four

3 packages tofu, about 8 oz/
    225 g each (drained weight)

4½ oz/125 g boneless pork

1 leek

few small dried whole chilies,
    soaked

vegetable oil, for deep-frying

1–2 scallions, cut into sections

2 tbsp crushed yellow bean sauce

1 tbsp light soy sauce

2 tsp rice wine or dry sherry

few drops of sesame oil

NUTRITION

Calories 218		Sugars 1g	
Protein 17g		Fat 16g	
Carbohydrate 2g		Saturates 2g	

1 Split each package of tofu into 3 slices crosswise, then cut each slice diagonally into 2 triangles.

2 Cut the pork into small thin slices or shreds. Cut the leek into thin strips.

COOK'S TIP

Tofu is sold in three forms: firm tofu, which can be smoked, silken tofu, or marinated tofu. It is the solid kind that is used for braising and stir-frying. Silken tofu is usually added to soups or sauces.

3 Drain the chilies and remove the seeds using the tip of a knife and discard, then cut into small shreds.

4 Heat the vegetable oil in a preheated wok until smoking, then deep-fry the tofu triangles for 2–3 minutes, or until golden brown all over. Remove with a slotted spoon and drain on paper towels.

5 Pour off the hot oil, leaving about 1 tablespoon in the wok. Add the pork strips, scallions, and chilies and stir-fry for 1 minute, or until the pork changes color.

6 Add the leek, tofu, yellow bean sauce, soy sauce, and wine and cook for 2–3 minutes, stirring gently to blend well. Sprinkle over the sesame oil and serve immediately.

charbroiled vegetables

serves four

1 large red bell pepper

1 large green bell pepper

1 large orange bell pepper

1 large zucchini

4 baby eggplants

2 red onions

2 tbsp lemon juice

1 tbsp olive oil

1 garlic clove, crushed

1 tbsp chopped fresh rosemary or
   1 tsp dried rosemary

salt and pepper

Fresh Tomato Relish (see page 103),
   to serve

NUTRITION

Calories 66	Sugars 7g
Protein 2g	Fat 3g
Carbohydrate 7g	Saturates 0.5g

1 Preheat the grill or broiler. Halve and seed the bell peppers. Cut into pieces 1 inch/2.5 cm wide.

2 Cut the zucchini in half lengthwise and slice into 1-inch/2.5-cm pieces. Place the bell peppers and zucchini in a bowl.

3 Cut the eggplants into fourths lengthwise. Cut the onions into 8 even-size wedges. Add the eggplants and onions to the bell peppers and zucchini.

4 Whisk the lemon juice, oil, garlic, and rosemary together in a small bowl. Season to taste with salt and pepper. Pour the mixture over the vegetables and stir to coat them evenly.

5 Thread the vegetables onto 8 metal or presoaked wooden skewers. Cook over hot coals, turning frequently, for 8–10 minutes, or until softened and beginning to char. Alternatively, arrange the kabobs on the broiler rack and cook under the hot broiler, turning frequently, for 10–12 minutes, or until the vegetables are lightly charred and just softened.

6 Drain the vegetable kabobs and serve them immediately, accompanied by Fresh Tomato Relish.

189

eggplant bake

serves four

3–4 tbsp olive oil

2 garlic cloves, crushed

2 large eggplants

3½ oz/100 g mozzarella cheese,
   thinly sliced

generous ¾ cup strained tomatoes

½ cup freshly grated
   Parmesan cheese

mixed salad greens, to serve

NUTRITION	
Calories 232	Sugars 8g
Protein 10g	Fat 18g
Carbohydrate 8g	Saturates 6g

1 Preheat the oven to 400°F/200°C. Heat 2 tablespoons of the oil in a large heavy-bottom skillet. Add the garlic and cook, stirring constantly, for 30 seconds.

2 Slice the eggplants lengthwise. Add the slices to the pan and cook for 3–4 minutes on each side, or until tender. (You will probably have to cook them in batches, so add the remaining oil as necessary.)

3 Remove the eggplants from the pan and drain on paper towels.

4 Place a layer of eggplant in a shallow ovenproof dish. Cover with a layer of mozzarella cheese, then pour over a third of the strained tomatoes. Continue layering in the same order, finishing with a layer of strained tomatoes on top.

5 Generously sprinkle the grated Parmesan cheese over the top and bake in the preheated oven for 25–30 minutes.

6 Transfer to serving plates and let cool, then serve warm or cold with salad greens.

asparagus packages

serves four

3½ oz/100 g fine tip asparagus

1 red bell pepper, seeded and
   thinly sliced

1 cup bean sprouts

2 tbsp plum sauce

1 egg yolk

8 sheets phyllo pastry

corn oil, for deep-frying

chili dipping sauce, to serve

NUTRITION

Calories 194		Sugars 2g
Protein 3g		Fat 16g
Carbohydrate 11g		Saturates 4g

1 Place the asparagus, bell pepper, and bean sprouts in a large bowl. Add the plum sauce to the vegetables and mix well.

2 Beat the egg yolk in a small bowl and reserve until required.

3 Lay the sheets of phyllo pastry out on a clean counter and cover with a damp dish towel to prevent them drying out.

4 Working with 1 sheet of phyllo pastry at a time, place a small quantity of the asparagus and bell pepper filling at the top end of the sheet. Brush all the edges of the phyllo pastry with a little of the beaten egg yolk. Roll up the sheet, tucking in the ends to enclose the filling like a spring roll. Continue filling and rolling the remaining phyllo pastry sheets.

5 Heat the oil for deep-frying in a preheated wok. Carefully cook the packages, 2 at a time, in the hot oil for 4–5 minutes, or until crispy.

6 Remove the packages with a slotted spoon and let drain on paper towels. Transfer the packages to warmed serving plates and serve immediately with a chili dipping sauce.

bell peppers with chestnuts

serves four

8 oz/225 g leeks

corn oil, for deep-frying

1 yellow bell pepper, seeded
and diced

1 green bell pepper, seeded and diced

1 red bell pepper, seeded and diced

7 oz/200 g canned water chestnuts,
drained and sliced

2 garlic cloves, crushed

3 tbsp light soy sauce

NUTRITION

Calories 192	Sugars 5g
Protein 3g	Fat 14g
Carbohydrate 13g	Saturates 13g

1 Thinly shred the leeks. Heat the oil for deep-frying in a preheated wok or large heavy-bottom pan.

2 Add the leeks to the wok and cook for 2–3 minutes, or until crispy. Remove with a slotted spoon and drain on paper towels. Reserve.

3 Pour all but 3 tablespoons of the oil from the wok. Add the yellow, green, and red bell peppers and stir-fry over high heat for 5 minutes, or until they begin to brown at the edges and have softened.

4 Add the water chestnuts, garlic, and soy sauce to the wok and stir-fry the vegetables for an additional 2–3 minutes.

5 Spoon the stir-fry onto warmed serving plates, then sprinkle with the reserved crispy leek and serve.

mixed bean pan-fry

serves four

12 oz/350 g mixed fresh beans,
    such as green and fava beans

2 tbsp vegetable oil

2 garlic cloves, crushed

1 red onion, halved and sliced

8 oz/225 g marinated tofu pieces
    (drained weight)

1 tbsp lemon juice

½ tsp ground turmeric

1 tsp ground allspice

⅔ cup vegetable stock

2 tsp sesame seeds

NUTRITION

Calories 179		Sugars 4g	
Protein 10g		Fat 11g	
Carbohydrate 10g		Saturates 1g	

VARIATION

Add lime juice instead of lemon
for an alternative citrus flavor.
Use smoked tofu instead of
marinated tofu, if you prefer.

1 Slice the green beans, then shell the fava beans and reserve until required.

2 Heat the oil in a large skillet. Add the garlic and onion and cook for 2 minutes, stirring well.

3 Add the tofu and cook for 2–3 minutes, or until just beginning to brown.

4 Add the reserved green beans and fava beans. Stir in the lemon juice, turmeric, allspice, and stock and bring to a boil.

5 Reduce the heat and simmer for 5–7 minutes, or until the beans are tender. Sprinkle with sesame seeds and serve immediately.

vegetable stir-fry with eggs

serves four

2 eggs

8 oz/225 g carrots

12 oz/350 g white cabbage

2 tbsp vegetable oil

1 red bell pepper, seeded and
   thinly sliced

3 cups fresh bean sprouts

1 tbsp tomato ketchup

2 tbsp soy sauce

½ cup salted peanuts, chopped

peanut sauce, to serve

NUTRITION

Calories 269	Sugars 12g
Protein 12g	Fat 19g
Carbohydrate 14g	Saturates 3g

COOK'S TIP

The eggs are cooled in cold
water after cooking in order to
prevent the egg yolks turning
black around the edges.

1 Bring a small pan of water to a
boil. Add the eggs and cook for
7 minutes. Remove the eggs from the
pan and cool under cold running water
for 1 minute. Shell the eggs, then cut
into fourths.

2 Coarsely grate the carrots and
finely shred the cabbage. Heat
the oil in a preheated wok or large
heavy-bottom skillet.

3 Add the carrots, cabbage, and
bell pepper to the wok and stir-fry
for 3 minutes.

4 Add the bean sprouts to the wok
and stir-fry for 2 minutes.

5 Mix the ketchup and soy sauce
together in a small bowl and add
to the wok, stirring well to combine.

6 Add the chopped peanuts to the
wok and stir-fry for 1 minute.

7 Transfer the stir-fry to warmed
serving plates and garnish with
the hard-cooked egg fourths. Serve
with a peanut sauce.

vegetable chop suey

serves four

1 yellow bell pepper, seeded

1 red bell pepper, seeded

1 carrot

1 zucchini

1 fennel bulb

1 onion

generous ½ cup snow peas

2 tbsp peanut oil

3 garlic cloves, crushed

1 tsp grated fresh gingerroot

2 cups bean sprouts

2 tsp brown sugar

2 tbsp light soy sauce

½ cup vegetable stock

NUTRITION

Calories 155	Sugars 6g
Protein 4g	Fat 12g
Carbohydrate 9g	Saturates 2g

1 Cut the bell peppers, carrot, zucchini, and fennel into thin slices. Cut the onion into fourths, then cut each fourth in half. Slice the snow peas diagonally to create the maximum surface area.

2 Heat the oil in a preheated wok. Add the garlic and ginger and stir-fry for 30 seconds. Add the onion and stir-fry for an additional 30 seconds.

VARIATION

Use any combination of colorful vegetables that you have to hand to make this versatile dish.

3 Add the bell peppers, carrot, zucchini, fennel, and snow peas to the wok and stir-fry for 2 minutes.

4 Add the bean sprouts to the wok and stir in the sugar, soy sauce, and stock. Reduce the heat to low and simmer for 1–2 minutes, or until the vegetables are tender and coated in the sauce.

5 Transfer the vegetables and sauce to a serving dish and serve immediately.

dolmades

8 oz/225 g grape leaves preserved
   in brine, about 40 in total

⅔ cup olive oil

4 tbsp lemon juice

1¼ cups water

lemon wedges, to serve

FILLING

generous ½ cup long-grain rice,
   not basmati

1½ cups water

salt and pepper

generous ⅓ cup currants

½ cup pine nuts, chopped

2 scallions, very finely chopped

1 tbsp very finely chopped
   cilantro

1 tbsp very finely chopped
   fresh parsley

1 tbsp very finely chopped fresh dill

finely grated rind of ½ lemon

NUTRITION

Calories 82	Sugars 2g
Protein 1g	Fat 7g
Carbohydrate 5g	Saturates 1g

1 Rinse the vine leaves in cold water and place them in a heatproof bowl. Cover with boiling water and soak for 5 minutes. Drain.

2 To make the filling, place the rice and water in a pan. Add a pinch of salt and cook for 10–12 minutes, or until the liquid is absorbed. Drain and let cool.

3 Stir the currants, pine nuts, scallions, herbs, lemon rind, and salt and pepper to taste into the rice.

4 Line the bottom of a large skillet with 3–4 of the thickest grape leaves or with any that are torn. Place a grape leaf on the counter, vein-side upward, with the pointed end facing away from you. Place a small, compact roll of the rice filling at the base of the leaf. Fold up the bottom end of the leaf.

5 Fold in each side of the leaf to overlap in the center. Roll up the leaf around the filling and squeeze lightly in your hand to shape and seal it. Continue with the remaining grape leaves and filling mixture.

6 Place the rolls in a single layer in the skillet, seam-side down. Combine the oil, lemon juice, and water and pour into the pan.

7 Fit a heatproof plate over the rolls and cover the skillet. Simmer for 30 minutes, then remove the skillet from the heat and let the stuffed grape leaves cool in the liquid. Serve chilled with lemon wedges.

cantonese garden vegetables

serves four

2 tbsp peanut oil

1 tsp Chinese five-spice powder

2¾ oz/75 g baby carrots, halved

2 celery stalks, sliced

2 baby leeks, sliced

½ cup snow peas

4 baby zucchini, halved lengthwise

8 baby corn cobs

8 oz/225 g marinated tofu pieces (drained weight)

4 tbsp fresh orange juice

1 tbsp clear honey

TO GARNISH

celery leaves

orange zest

NUTRITION

Calories 130	Sugars 8g
Protein 6g	Fat 8g
Carbohydrate 8g	Saturates 1g

1 Heat the oil in a preheated wok until almost smoking. Add the five-spice powder, carrots, celery, leeks, snow peas, zucchini, and baby corn cobs and stir-fry for 3–4 minutes.

2 Add the tofu and cook for an additional 2 minutes, stirring.

3 Stir in the orange juice and honey, then reduce the heat and stir-fry for 1–2 minutes.

4 Transfer the stir-fry to a serving dish and garnish with celery leaves and orange zest. Serve immediately.

COOK'S TIP

Chinese five-spice powder is a mixture of fennel, star anise, cinnamon bark, cloves, and Szechuan pepper. It is very pungent, so it should be used sparingly. If kept in an airtight container, it will keep indefinitely.

oven-baked risotto

serves four

4 tbsp olive oil

14 oz/400 g portobello mushrooms, thickly sliced

4 oz/115 g pancetta or thick-cut smoked bacon, diced

1 large onion, finely chopped

2 garlic cloves, finely chopped

1¾ cups risotto rice

1 quart chicken stock, simmering

2 tbsp chopped fresh tarragon or flatleaf parsley

salt and pepper

¾ cup freshly grated Parmesan cheese, plus extra for sprinkling

NUTRITION

Calories 428	Sugars 2g
Protein 15g	Fat 18g
Carbohydrate 14g	Saturates 6g

1 Preheat the oven to 350°F/180°C. Heat 2 tablespoons of the oil in a large heavy-bottom skillet over high heat. Add the mushrooms and stir-fry for 2–3 minutes, or until golden and tender. Transfer to a plate.

2 Add the pancetta to the skillet and cook for 2 minutes, stirring frequently, until crisp and golden. Remove with a slotted spoon and add to the mushrooms on the plate.

3 Heat the remaining oil in a heavy-bottom pan over medium heat. Add the onion and cook for 2 minutes. Add the garlic and rice and cook, stirring, for 2 minutes, or until the rice is well coated with the oil.

4 Gradually stir the stock into the rice, then add the mushroom and pancetta mixture and the tarragon. Season to taste with salt and pepper. Bring to a boil.

5 Remove the pan from the heat and transfer to a casserole.

6 Cover and bake in the preheated oven for 20 minutes, or until the rice is almost tender and most of the liquid has been absorbed. Uncover and stir in the Parmesan cheese. Bake for an additional 15 minutes, or until the rice is tender but still firm to the bite. Serve immediately with extra Parmesan cheese for sprinkling.

baked eggplant gratin

serves four–six

1 large eggplant, about
  1 lb 12 oz/800 g
10½ oz/300 g mozzarella cheese
3 oz/85 g Parmesan cheese
olive oil
about 1 cup Tomato Sauce
  (see page 74) or good quality
  bottled tomato sauce for pasta
salt and pepper

NUTRITION	
Calories 261	Sugars 5g
Protein 20g	Fat 18g
Carbohydrate 6g	Saturates 10g

1 Trim the eggplant and, using a sharp knife, cut it into ¼-inch/5-mm slices crosswise. Arrange the eggplant slices on a large plate, then sprinkle with salt and let drain for 30 minutes.

2 Preheat the oven to 400°F/200°C. Drain and grate the mozzarella cheese and finely grate the Parmesan cheese.

3 Rinse the eggplant slices under cold running water and pat dry with paper towels. Lightly brush a cookie sheet with oil and arrange the eggplant slices in a single layer. Brush the tops with oil.

4 Roast in the preheated oven for 5 minutes. Using tongs, turn the slices over, then brush with a little more oil and bake for an additional 5 minutes, or until the eggplant is cooked through and tender. Do not turn off the oven.

5 Spread about 1 tablespoon of oil over the bottom of a gratin dish or other ovenproof serving dish. Add a layer of eggplant slices, about a fourth of the Tomato Sauce, and top with a fourth of the mozzarella. Season to taste with salt and pepper.

6 Continue layering until all the ingredients are used, ending with a layer of sauce. Sprinkle the Parmesan cheese over the top. Bake for 30 minutes, or until bubbling. Let stand for 5 minutes before serving.

tomato curry

serves four

14 oz/400 g canned tomatoes

1 tsp finely chopped fresh
   gingerroot

1 tsp crushed garlic

1 tsp chili powder

1 tsp salt

½ tsp ground coriander

½ tsp ground cumin

4 tbsp corn oil

½ tsp onion seeds

½ tsp mustard seeds

½ tsp fenugreek seeds

pinch of white cumin seeds

3 dried red chilies

2 tbsp lemon juice

3 hard-cooked eggs

cilantro leaves, to garnish

NUTRITION

Calories 170	Sugars 3g
Protein 6g	Fat 15g
Carbohydrate 3g	Saturates 2g

1 Place the tomatoes in a large bowl. Add the ginger, garlic, chili powder, salt, coriander, and ground cumin and blend well.

2 Heat the oil in a pan. Add the onion, mustard, fenugreek, and white cumin seeds, and the dried red chilies and stir-fry for 1 minute, or until they give off their aroma. Remove the pan from the heat.

3 Add the tomato mixture to the spicy oil mixture and return the pan to the heat. Stir-fry for 3 minutes.

4 Reduce the heat and continue to cook, partially covered and stirring frequently, for 7–10 minutes.

5 Sprinkle over 1 tablespoon of the lemon juice. Taste and add the remaining lemon juice if required.

6 Transfer the tomato curry to a warmed serving dish and keep warm until required.

7 Shell the hard-cooked eggs and cut them into fourths. Add them to the tomato curry, pushing them in gently, yolk-end downward. Garnish with cilantro leaves and serve.

creamy stuffed mushrooms

serves four

1 oz/25 g dried cèpes

8 oz/225 g mealy potatoes, diced

salt and pepper

2 tbsp butter, melted

4 tbsp heavy cream

2 tbsp snipped fresh chives

8 large open-cap mushrooms

¼ cup grated Emmental cheese

⅔ cup vegetable stock

fresh chives, to garnish

salad greens, to serve

1 Preheat the oven to 425°F/220°C. Place the dried cèpes in a small heatproof bowl. Pour over enough boiling water to cover and let soak for 20 minutes.

2 Meanwhile, cook the potatoes in a pan of lightly salted boiling water for 10 minutes, or until cooked through and tender. Drain them well and mash until smooth.

3 Drain the soaked cèpes and chop them finely. Mix them into the mashed potato.

4 Thoroughly blend the butter, cream, and chives together in a pitcher and pour the mixture into the potato mixture, stirring well to blend. Season to taste with salt and pepper.

5 Remove the stems from the open-cap mushrooms. Chop the stems and stir them into the potato mixture. Spoon the mixture into the open-cap mushrooms and sprinkle the grated cheese over the top.

6 Arrange the filled mushrooms in a shallow ovenproof dish and pour the stock around them.

7 Cover the dish and cook in the preheated oven for 20 minutes. Remove the lid and cook for an additional 5 minutes, or until the tops are golden.

8 Garnish with chives and serve with salad greens.

NUTRITION

Calories 214	Sugars 1g
Protein 5g	Fat 17g
Carbohydrate 11g	Saturates 11g

broccoli in oyster sauce

serves four

9–10½ oz/250–300 g broccoli

3 tbsp vegetable oil

3–4 small slices fresh gingerroot

½ tsp salt

½ tsp sugar

3–4 tbsp water

1 tbsp oyster sauce

NUTRITION

Calories 100	Sugars 1g
Protein 3g	Fat 9g
Carbohydrate 2g	Saturates 1g

COOK'S TIP

The broccoli stems have to be peeled and cut diagonally to ensure that they will cook evenly. If they are thin stems, the pieces can be added to the wok at the same time as the florets, but otherwise add the stems first, to ensure that they will be tender.

1 Using a sharp knife, cut the broccoli spears into small florets. Trim the stems and peel off the rough skin, then cut the stems diagonally into diamond-shaped chunks.

2 Heat the oil in a preheated wok until really hot.

3 Add the pieces of broccoli stem and the slices of ginger to the wok and stir-fry for 30 seconds, then add the florets and continue to stir-fry for an additional 2 minutes.

4 Add the salt, sugar, and water, and stir-fry for an additional 1 minute.

5 Blend in the oyster sauce. Transfer the broccoli to a serving dish and serve hot or cold.

spinach frittata

serves four

1 lb/450 g fresh spinach leaves

2 tsp water

4 eggs, beaten

2 tbsp light cream

2 garlic cloves, crushed

⅓ cup canned corn kernels,
   drained

1 celery stalk, chopped

1 fresh red chili, seeded
   and chopped

2 tomatoes, seeded and diced

2 tbsp olive oil

2 tbsp butter

4 tbsp pecan nut halves

2 tbsp grated romano cheese

1 oz/25 g fontina cheese, cubed

pinch of paprika

COOK'S TIP

Be careful not to burn the
underside of the frittata during
the initial cooking stage—this is
why it is important to use a
heavy-bottom skillet. Add a
little extra oil to the pan when
you turn the frittata over,
if required.

1 Cook the spinach in the water in a covered pan for 5 minutes. Drain thoroughly and pat dry on paper towels.

2 Beat the eggs in a bowl and stir in the spinach, cream, garlic, corn, celery, chili, and tomatoes until the ingredients are well mixed together.

NUTRITION

Calories 307	Sugars 4g
Protein 15g	Fat 25g
Carbohydrate 6g	Saturates 8g

3 Heat the oil and butter in an 8-inch/20-cm heavy-bottom skillet over medium heat.

4 Spoon the egg mixture into the skillet and sprinkle with the pecan nut halves, romano and fontina cheeses, and paprika. Cook, without stirring, over medium heat for 5–7 minutes, or until the underside of the frittata is brown.

5 Place a large plate over the skillet and invert to turn out the frittata. Slide it back into the skillet and cook the other side for an additional 2–3 minutes. Serve the frittata straight from the skillet or transfer to a serving plate and serve immediately.

ratatouille

serves four–six

1 large eggplant, about
10½ oz/300 g

salt and pepper

5 tbsp olive oil

2 large onions, thinly sliced

2 large garlic cloves, crushed

4 zucchini, sliced

1 lb 12 oz/800 g canned
chopped tomatoes

1 tsp sugar

1 bouquet garni of 2 fresh
thyme sprigs, 2 large fresh
parsley sprigs, 1 fresh basil sprig,
and 1 bay leaf, tied in a 3-inch/
7.5-cm piece of celery

fresh basil leaves, to garnish

NUTRITION

Calories 157	Sugars 11g
Protein 4g	Fat 9g
Carbohydrate 14g	Saturates 1g

1 Coarsely chop the eggplant, then place in a colander. Sprinkle with salt and let stand for 30 minutes to drain. Rinse well under cold running water to remove all traces of the salt and pat dry with paper towels.

2 Heat the oil in a large heavy-bottom flameproof casserole over medium heat. Add the onions, then reduce the heat and cook, stirring occasionally, for 10 minutes, or until softened and light golden brown.

3 Add the garlic and cook for an additional 2 minutes, or until the onions are tender.

4 Add the eggplant, zucchini, tomatoes with their can juices, sugar, and bouquet garni. Season to taste with salt and pepper. Bring to a boil, then reduce the heat to very low and simmer, covered, for 30 minutes.

5 Taste and adjust the seasoning if necessary. Remove and discard the bouquet garni. Garnish the vegetable stew with basil leaves and serve immediately.

spinach & herb frittata

serves six–eight

4 tbsp olive oil

6 scallions, sliced

9 oz/250 g young spinach
  leaves, any coarse stems
  removed, rinsed

6 large eggs

salt and pepper

3 tbsp finely chopped mixed fresh
  herbs, such as flatleaf parsley,
  thyme, and cilantro

2 tbsp freshly grated Parmesan
  cheese, plus extra for garnishing

fresh parsley sprigs, to garnish

NUTRITION	
Calories 145	Sugars 1g
Protein 8g	Fat 12g
Carbohydrate 1g	Saturates 13g

1 Preheat the broiler. Heat a 10-inch/25-cm skillet, preferably nonstick with a flameproof handle, over medium heat. Add the oil and heat. Add the scallions and cook for 2 minutes.

2 Add the spinach and cook until it is just wilted.

3 Beat the eggs and season to taste with salt and pepper. Using a slotted spoon, transfer the spinach and onions to the eggs and stir in the herbs. Pour the excess oil left in the skillet into a heatproof pitcher, then scrape off the bits from the bottom of the pan.

4 Reheat the skillet. Add 2 tablespoons of the reserved oil. Pour in the egg mixture, smoothing it into an even layer. Cook, shaking the skillet occasionally, for 6 minutes, or until the bottom is set when you lift up the side with a spatula.

5 Sprinkle the top of the frittata with the Parmesan cheese. Place the pan under the hot broiler and cook for 3 minutes, or until the excess liquid is set and the cheese is golden.

6 Remove the skillet from the heat and slide the frittata out onto a warm serving plate. Let the frittata stand for at least 5 minutes before cutting and garnishing with extra Parmesan cheese and parsley. The frittata can be served hot, warm, or at room temperature.

thai-spiced mushrooms

serves four

8 large flat mushrooms

3 tbsp corn oil

2 tbsp light soy sauce

1 garlic clove, crushed

¾-inch/2-cm piece fresh galangal or
    gingerroot, grated

1 tbsp Thai green curry paste

8 baby corn cobs, sliced

3 scallions, chopped

2 cups bean sprouts

3½ oz/100 g firm tofu (drained
    weight), diced

2 tsp sesame seeds, toasted

TO SERVE

chopped cucumber

sliced red bell pepper

NUTRITION

Calories 147	Sugars 2g
Protein 6g	Fat 12g
Carbohydrate 4g	Saturates 1g

1 Preheat the broiler to high. Remove the stems from the mushrooms and reserve. Place the caps on a cookie sheet. Mix 2 tablespoons of the oil with 1 tablespoon of the soy sauce and brush over the mushrooms.

2 Cook the mushroom caps under the hot broiler until golden and tender, turning them over once.

3 Meanwhile, chop the mushroom stems finely. Heat the remaining oil in a large skillet or preheated wok. Add the mushroom stems, garlic, and galangal and stir-fry for 1 minute.

4 Stir in the curry paste, baby corn cobs, and scallions and stir-fry for 1 minute. Add the bean sprouts and stir-fry for an additional 1 minute.

5 Add the tofu and remaining soy sauce, then toss lightly to heat. Spoon the mixture into the mushroom caps.

6 Sprinkle with sesame seeds and serve with chopped cucumber and sliced red bell pepper.

vegetable rolls

serves four

8 large Napa cabbage leaves

FILLING

2 baby corn cobs, sliced

1 carrot, finely chopped

1 celery stalk, chopped

4 scallions, chopped

4 water chestnuts, chopped

2 tbsp unsalted cashews, chopped

1 garlic clove, chopped

1 tsp grated fresh gingerroot

1 oz/25 g canned bamboo shoots,
     drained, rinsed, and chopped

1 tsp sesame oil

2 tsp soy sauce

NUTRITION	
Calories 69	Sugars 1g
Protein 2g	Fat 5g
Carbohydrate 3g	Saturates 1g

1 Place the Napa cabbage leaves in a large heatproof bowl and pour over boiling water to soften them. Let them stand for 1 minute and drain thoroughly.

2 Mix the baby corn cobs, carrot, celery, scallions, water chestnuts, cashew nuts, garlic, ginger, and bamboo shoots together in a large bowl.

3 Whisk the oil and soy sauce together in a separate bowl. Add this to the vegetables and stir well until all the vegetables are thoroughly coated in the mixture.

4 Spread out the Napa cabbage leaves on a cutting board and divide the filling mixture between them, carefully spooning an equal quantity of the mixture on to each leaf.

5 Roll up the Napa cabbage leaves, folding in the sides, to make neat packages. Secure the packages with wooden toothpicks.

6 Place in a small heatproof dish in a steamer, then cover and cook for 15–20 minutes, or until the packages are cooked.

7 Transfer the vegetable rolls to a warmed serving dish and serve immediately.

Desserts

You can still enjoy a dessert or a sweet treat on a low-carbohydrate diet, as the following recipes prove. Some, of course, are higher in

carbs than others, so be sure to consult the nutritional information alongside each recipe when making your choice, so that you can limit the "naughtier" ones to an occasional indulgence.

As with vegetables, eating as wide a variety of fruits as possible is the healthy approach, and here you can feast on luscious summer berries in Balsamic Strawberries (see page 216), fragrant tropical fruits in Pineapple with Tequila & Mint (see page 250), and no less enticing tree fruits in Peaches in White Wine (see page 234) and Figs with Orange Cream. (see page 232)

But if a hit of chocolate is what you crave, try the moreish Mini Florentines (see page 221), or the truly wicked Rich Chocolate Loaf (see page 218).

balsamic strawberries

COOK'S TIP

This is most enjoyable when it is
made with the best quality
balsamic vinegar, one that has
aged slowly and has turned thick
and syrupy. Unfortunately, the
genuine mixture is always
expensive—cheaper versions are
artificially sweetened
and colored.

1 Wipe the strawberries with a
damp cloth, rather than rinsing
them, so they do not become soggy.
Using a paring knife, cut off the stems
at the top, then use the tip to remove
the core.

2 Cut each strawberry in half or into
fourths if large. Transfer to a large
nonmetallic bowl.

3 Add ½ tablespoon of the vinegar
per person. Add several twists of
pepper, then gently stir together. Cover
with plastic wrap and let chill in the
refrigerator for 4 hours.

4 Just before serving, stir in the
mint leaves to taste. Spoon the
mascarpone cheese into bowls and
spoon the berries on top.

5 Decorate the balsamic
strawberries with a few mint
leaves, if desired. Sprinkle with extra
pepper to taste.

rich chocolate loaf

makes sixteen slices

½ cup whole almonds

5 squares semisweet chocolate

6 tbsp unsalted butter

generous ¾ cup condensed milk

2 tsp ground cinnamon

3 oz/85 g amaretti cookies, broken

⅓ cup no-soak dried apricots,
   coarsely chopped

NUTRITION

Calories 118	Sugars 16g
Protein 3g	Fat 12g
Carbohydrate 18g	Saturates 6g

COOK'S TIP

To melt chocolate, first break it into manageable pieces. The smaller the pieces, the quicker it will melt.

1 Line a 1-lb 8 oz/675-g loaf pan with a sheet of foil.

2 Using a sharp knife, coarsely chop the almonds.

3 Place the chocolate, butter, condensed milk, and cinnamon in a heavy-bottom pan.

4 Heat the chocolate mixture over low heat for 3–4 minutes, stirring constantly with a wooden spoon, until the chocolate has melted. Beat the mixture well.

5 Stir the chopped almonds, broken cookies, and apricots into the chocolate mixture, stirring with a wooden spoon until well mixed.

6 Pour the mixture into the prepared pan. Cover and let chill in the refrigerator for 1 hour, or until set. Cut the loaf into slices to serve.

coconut candy

serves four–six

scant ¾ stick butter

2 cups dry unsweetened coconut

¾ cup condensed milk

few drops of pink food coloring
   (optional)

NUTRITION

Calories 338	Sugars 5g
Protein 4g	Fat 34g
Carbohydrate 5g	Saturates 26g

COOK'S TIP

Coconut is used extensively in Indian cooking to add flavor and creaminess to various dishes. The best flavor comes from freshly grated coconut, although ready-prepared dry unsweetened coconut, as used here, makes an excellent standby. Freshly grated coconut freezes successfully, so it is well worth preparing when you have the time.

1 Place the butter in a heavy-bottom pan and melt over low heat, stirring constantly.

2 Add the coconut to the melted butter, stirring to mix.

3 Stir in the condensed milk and the food coloring, if using, and mix constantly for 7–10 minutes.

4 Remove the pan from the heat and let the coconut mixture cool slightly.

5 Once cool enough to handle, shape the coconut mixture into long blocks and cut into equal-size rectangles. Let set for 1 hour, then serve.

mini florentines

makes forty

6 tbsp butter, plus extra for greasing

all-purpose flour, for dusting

generous ⅓ cup superfine sugar

2 tbsp golden raisins or raisins

2 tbsp chopped candied cherries

2 tbsp chopped candied ginger

¼ cup sunflower seeds

scant 1 cup slivered almonds

2 tbsp heavy cream

6 squares semisweet chocolate

NUTRITION	
Calories 75	Sugars 6g
Protein 1g	Fat 5g
Carbohydrate 6g	Saturates 2g

1 Preheat the oven to 350°F/180°C. Grease and flour 2 cookie sheets.

2 Place the butter in a pan and heat until melted. Add the sugar and stir until dissolved, then bring to a boil. Remove from the heat and stir in the golden raisins, cherries, ginger, sunflower seeds, and almonds. Mix well, then beat in the cream.

3 Place small teaspoons of the fruit and nut mixture onto the prepared cookie sheets, leaving plenty of space for the mixture to spread. Bake in the preheated oven for 10–12 minutes, or until light golden.

4 Remove from the oven and, while still hot, use a circular cookie cutter to pull in the edges to form perfect circles. Let cool and go crisp before removing from the cookie sheets.

5 Break the chocolate into pieces, then place in a heatproof bowl over a pan of simmering water and stir until melted. Spread most of the chocolate onto a sheet of parchment paper. When the chocolate is on the point of setting, place the cookies flat-side down on the chocolate and let it harden completely.

6 Cut around the florentines and remove from the parchment paper. Spread a little more melted chocolate on the coated side of the florentines and use a fork to mark waves in the chocolate. Let set. Arrange the florentines on a plate (or in a presentation box for a gift) with alternate sides facing upward. Keep them cool.

lavender hearts

makes about forty-eight

1½ cups all-purpose flour, plus extra
   for dusting
scant ¾ stick chilled butter, diced
generous ⅓ cup superfine sugar
1 large egg
1 tbsp dried lavender flowers, very
   finely chopped
TO DECORATE
about 4 tbsp confectioners' sugar
about 1 tsp cold water
about 2 tbsp fresh lavender flowers

NUTRITION

Calories 36		Sugars 2g	
Protein 1g		Fat 1g	
Carbohydrate 5g		Saturates 1g	

1 Preheat the oven to 350°F/180°C. Line 2 cookie sheets with parchment paper. Place the flour in a bowl, then add the butter and cut it in until the mixture resembles bread crumbs. Stir in the superfine sugar.

2 Lightly beat the egg, then add it to the flour and butter mixture along with the dried lavender flowers. Stir the mixture until a stiff paste is formed.

3 Turn out the dough onto a lightly floured counter and roll out until about ¼ inch/5 mm thick.

4 Using a 2-inch/5-cm heart-shaped cookie cutter, press out 48 cookies, occasionally dipping the cutter into extra flour, and re-rolling the trimmings as necessary. Transfer the pastry hearts to the cookie sheets.

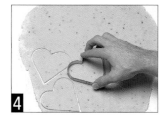

5 Prick the surface of each heart with a fork. Bake in the preheated oven for 10 minutes, or until lightly browned. Transfer to a wire rack set over parchment paper to cool.

6 Sift the confectioners' sugar into a bowl. Add the water and stir until a thin, smooth frosting forms, adding a little extra water if necessary.

7 Drizzle the frosting from the tip of the spoon over the cooled cookies in a random pattern. Immediately sprinkle with the fresh lavender flowers while the frosting is still soft so that they stick in place. Let stand for at least 15 minutes, or until the frosting has set. Store the cookies for up to 4 days in an airtight container.

zabaglione

4 egg yolks

⅓ cup superfine sugar

½ cup Marsala wine

amaretti cookies, to serve (optional)

NUTRITION

Calories 110		Sugars 13g	
Protein 2g		Fat 4g	
Carbohydrate 13g		Saturates 1g	

COOK'S TIP

Decorate the zabaglione
with a slit strawberry,
placed on the rim of the glass,
or serve with ladyfingers
or crisp cookies.

1 Half fill a pan with water and bring to a boil. Reduce the heat so that the water is barely simmering.

2 Beat the egg yolks and sugar together in a heatproof bowl with an electric whisk until pale and creamy. Set the bowl over the pan of water. Do not let the bottom of the bowl touch the surface of the water, or the egg yolks will scramble.

3 Gradually add the Marsala wine, beating constantly with the electric whisk. Continue beating until the mixture is thick and has increased in volume. Pour into heatproof glasses or bowls and serve immediately with amaretti cookies.

italian chocolate truffles

makes twenty-four

6 squares semisweet chocolate

2 tbsp almond-flavored liqueur or
   orange-flavored liqueur

3 tbsp unsalted butter

scant ½ cup confectioners' sugar

½ cup ground almonds

1¾ squares milk chocolate, grated

NUTRITION	
Calories 82	Sugars 7g
Protein 1g	Fat 5g
Carbohydrate 8g	Saturates 3g

1 Melt the semisweet chocolate with the liqueur in a heatproof bowl set over a pan of hot water, stirring until well combined.

2 Add the butter and stir until it has melted. Stir in the sugar and the ground almonds.

3 Let the mixture stand in a cool place until firm enough to roll into 24 balls.

4 Place the grated milk chocolate on a plate and roll the truffles in the chocolate to coat them.

5 Place the truffles in paper candy cases and let chill.

VARIATION

Almond-flavored liqueur gives these truffles an authentic Italian flavor. The original almond liqueur, Amaretto di Saronno, comes from Saronno in Italy.

exotic fruit packages

serves four

1 papaya

1 mango

1 carambola

1 tbsp grenadine

3 tbsp orange juice

lowfat plain yogurt or light cream,
   to serve

NUTRITION	
Calories 43	Sugars 9g
Protein 2g	Fat 0.3g
Carbohydrate 9g	Saturates 0.1g

1 Cut the papaya in half, then scoop out the seeds and discard them. Peel the papaya and cut the flesh into thick slices.

2 Prepare the mango by cutting it in half lengthwise and cutting carefully away from the flat central pit with a sharp knife.

3 Score each mango half in a criss-cross pattern. Push each mango half inside out to separate the cubes, and cut them away from the skin.

4 Using a sharp knife, thickly slice the carambola.

5 Place all the fruits in a bowl and mix them together.

6 Mix the grenadine and orange juice together and pour over the fruits. Let marinate for at least 30 minutes.

7 Preheat the grill. Divide the fruits between 4 double-thickness squares of foil and gather the edges to form a package that encloses the fruits.

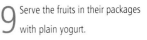

8 Place the foil packages on a rack set over warm coals and cook for 15–20 minutes.

9 Serve the fruits in their packages with plain yogurt.

rose ice

serves four

1¾ cups water

2 tbsp coconut cream

4 tbsp sweetened condensed milk

2 tsp rose water

few drops of pink food coloring
  (optional)

pink rose petals, to decorate

NUTRITION	
Calories 76	Sugars 9g
Protein 2g	Fat 4g
Carbohydrate 9g	Saturates 3g

COOK'S TIP

To prevent the ice thawing too quickly at the table, nestle the bottom of the serving dish in another dish filled with crushed ice.

1 Place the water in a small pan and add the coconut cream. Heat the mixture gently without boiling, stirring constantly.

2 Remove from the heat and let cool. Stir in the sweetened condensed milk, rose water, and food coloring, if using.

3 Pour into a freezerproof container and freeze for 1–1½ hours, or until slushy.

4 Remove from the freezer and break up the ice crystals with a fork. Return to the freezer and freeze until firm.

5 Spoon the ice roughly into a pile on a serving dish and sprinkle with rose petals to decorate.

mocha swirl mousse

serves four

1 tbsp coffee and chicory extract

2 tsp unsweetened cocoa, plus extra
  for dusting

1 tsp lowfat drinking
  chocolate powder

⅔ cup lowfat sour cream, plus 4 tsp
  to serve

2 tsp powdered gelozone
  (vegetarian gelatin)

2 tbsp boiling water

2 large egg whites

2 tbsp superfine sugar

4 chocolate coffee beans, to serve

NUTRITION

Calories 136		Sugars 5g
Protein 5g		Fat 8g
Carbohydrate 11g		Saturates 5g

COOK'S TIP

The vegetarian equivalent of
gelatin, called gelozone, is
available from healthfood stores.

1 Place the coffee and chicory
  extract in one bowl and the cocoa
and drinking chocolate in another
bowl. Divide the sour cream between
the 2 bowls and mix both well.

2 Dissolve the gelozone in the
  boiling water in a heatproof bowl
and reserve. Whisk the egg whites and
sugar in a greasefree bowl until stiff
and divide this evenly between the
2 mixtures.

3 Divide the dissolved gelozone
  between the 2 mixtures and,
using a large metal spoon, gently fold
in until well mixed.

4 Spoon small amounts of the
  2 mousses alternately into
4 serving glasses and swirl together
gently. Let chill in the refrigerator for
1 hour, or until set.

5 To serve, top each mousse
  with a teaspoonful of sour cream,
a chocolate coffee bean, and a light
dusting of cocoa.

figs with orange cream

serves four

8 large fresh figs

4 large fresh fig leaves, if available,
    rinsed and dried

CREME FRAICHE

2 tbsp buttermilk

1¼ cups heavy cream

ORANGE BLOSSOM CREAM

½ cup Crème Fraîche

about 4 tbsp orange blossom water

1 tsp orange blossom honey

finely grated rind of ½ orange

2 tbsp slivered almonds,
    to decorate (optional)

1 Begin making the Crème Fraîche at least a day ahead. Place the buttermilk in a preserving jar or a jar with a screw top. Add the cream, then close securely and shake to blend. Let stand at room temperature for 6–8 hours, or until set, then chill for at least 8 hours and up to 4 days. It will develop a slight tangy flavor. Lightly beat the Crème Fraîche before using.

2 To toast the almonds for the decoration, place in a dry skillet over medium heat and stir until lightly browned. Take care that they do not burn. Immediately tip the almonds out of the pan. Reserve.

3 To make the Orange Blossom Cream, place the Crème Fraîche in a small bowl and stir in the orange blossom water with the orange blossom honey and orange rind. Taste and add a little extra orange blossom water if necessary.

4 To serve, cut the stems off the figs, but do not peel them. Stand the figs upright with the pointed end upward. Cut each fig into fourths without cutting all the way through, so that you can open them out into attractive "flowers."

5 If you are using fig leaves, place one in the center of each serving plate. Arrange 2 figs on top of each leaf and spoon a small amount of the orange-flavored cream alongside them. Sprinkle the cream with the toasted almonds, if desired, just before serving.

NUTRITION	
Calories 20	Sugars 13g
Protein 3g	Fat 18g
Carbohydrate 14g	Saturates 9g

paper-thin fruit pies

serves four

1 dessert apple

1 ripe pear

2 tbsp lemon juice

4 tbsp lowfat spread

8 oz/225 g phyllo pastry, thawed
   if frozen

2 tbsp low-sugar apricot jelly

1 tbsp unsweetened orange juice

1 tbsp finely chopped pistachio nuts

2 tsp confectioners' sugar, for dusting

lowfat custard, to serve

NUTRITION

Calories 158	Sugars 12g
Protein 2g	Fat 10g
Carbohydrate 14g	Saturates 2g

1 Preheat the oven to 400°F/200°C. Core and thinly slice the apple and pear and toss them in the lemon juice to prevent discoloration.

VARIATION

Other combinations of fruit are equally delicious. Try peach and apricot, raspberry, and apple, or pineapple and mango.

2 Melt the spread in a small pan over low heat. Cut the sheets of phyllo pastry into fourths and cover with a clean, damp dish towel. Brush 4 nonstick shallow pans, measuring 4 inches/10 cm across, with a little of the spread.

3 Working on each pie separately, brush 4 sheets of phyllo with spread. Press a small sheet of phyllo into the bottom of 1 pan. Arrange the other sheets of phyllo on top at slightly different angles. Repeat with the remaining sheets of phyllo to make another 3 pies. Arrange the apple and pear slices alternately in the center of each pastry shell and lightly crimp the edges of the dough of each pie.

4 Mix the jelly and orange juice together until smooth and brush over the fruits. Bake in the preheated oven for 12–15 minutes. Sprinkle with the pistachio nuts and dust lightly with sugar, then serve with custard.

peaches in white wine

serves four

4 large peaches

2 tbsp confectioners' sugar, sifted

1 orange

generous ¾ cup medium or sweet
　 white wine, chilled

NUTRITION

Calories 89	Sugars 14g
Protein 1g	Fat 0g
Carbohydrate 14g	Saturates 0g

COOK'S TIP

There is absolutely no need to
use expensive wine in this recipe,
so it can be quite economical
to make.

1 Using a sharp knife, halve the peaches, then remove the pits and discard them. Peel the peaches, if you prefer. Slice into thin wedges.

2 Place the peach wedges in a glass serving bowl and sprinkle over the sugar.

3 Using a sharp knife, pare the rind from the orange. Cut the orange rind into short thin sticks and place them in a bowl of cold water. Reserve.

4 Squeeze the juice from the orange and pour over the peaches, together with the chilled wine.

5 Cover and place the bowl in the refrigerator for at least 1 hour to let the peaches marinate and chill.

6 Remove the orange rind sticks from the water and pat them dry with paper towels.

7 Decorate the chilled marinated peaches with the strips of orange rind and serve immediately.

tropical salad

serves eight

1 papaya

2 tbsp fresh orange juice

3 tbsp rum

2 bananas

2 guavas

1 small pineapple or 2 baby
   pineapples

2 passion fruit

pineapple leaves, to decorate

NUTRITION

Calories 69	Sugars 13g
Protein 1g	Fat 0.3g
Carbohydrate 14g	Saturates 0g

COOK'S TIP

Guavas have a heavenly smell
when ripe—their scent will fill a
whole room. They should give to
gentle pressure when ripe, and
their skins should be yellow. The
canned varieties are very good
and have a pink tinge to
the flesh.

1 Cut the papaya in half and
remove and discard the seeds.
Peel and slice the flesh into a bowl.

2 Pour over the orange juice
together with the rum.

3 Peel and slice the bananas, and
peel and slice the guavas, then
add both to the bowl.

4 Cut the top and base from the
pineapple, then cut off the skin.

5 Slice the pineapple flesh,
discarding the core, then cut into
pieces and add to the bowl.

6 Halve the passion fruit and scoop
out the flesh with a teaspoon.
Add to the bowl and stir well to mix.

7 Spoon the salad into glass bowls
and decorate with pineapple
leaves. Serve.

chocolate biscotti

makes sixteen

butter, for greasing

1 egg

½ cup superfine sugar

1 tsp vanilla extract

scant 1 cup all-purpose flour, plus
extra for dusting

½ tsp baking powder

1 tsp ground cinnamon

1¾ squares semisweet chocolate,
coarsely chopped

scant ½ cup toasted slivered almonds

scant ½ cup pine nuts

NUTRITION

Calories 113	Sugars 9g
Protein 2g	Fat 5g
Carbohydrate 15g	Saturates 1g

1 Preheat the oven to 350°F/180°C. Grease a cookie sheet with butter.

2 Whisk the egg, sugar, and vanilla extract in a large bowl with an electric mixer until it is thick and pale—ribbons of mixture should trail from the whisk as you lift it.

3 Sift the flour, baking powder, and cinnamon into a separate bowl, then sift into the egg mixture and fold in gently. Stir in the chocolate, almonds, and pine nuts.

4 Turn out onto a floured counter and shape into a flat log 9 inches/23 cm long and ¾ inch/ 2 cm wide. Transfer to the prepared cookie sheet.

5 Bake in the preheated oven for 20–25 minutes, or until golden. Remove from the oven and let cool for 5 minutes, or until firm.

6 Transfer the log to a cutting board. Using a serrated bread knife, cut the log on the diagonal into slices about ½ inch/1 cm thick and arrange them on the cookie sheet. Cook for 10–15 minutes, turning halfway through the cooking time.

7 Let cool for 5 minutes. Transfer to a wire rack to cool completely.

creamy fruit parfait

serves four–six

8 oz/225 g cherries

2 large peaches

2 large apricots

3 cups strained plain yogurt or thick
   plain yogurt

½ cup walnut halves

2 tbsp flower-scented honey

fresh red currants or berries,
   to decorate (optional)

NUTRITION

Calories 261	Sugars 17g
Protein 10g	Fat 18g
Carbohydrate 17g	Saturates 7g

1 To prepare the fruits, use a cherry or olive pitter to remove the cherry pits. Cut each cherry in half. Cut the peaches and apricots in half from top to bottom and remove and discard the pits, then finely chop the flesh of all the fruits.

2 Place the finely chopped cherries, peaches, and apricots in a bowl and gently stir together.

3 Spoon one-third of the yogurt into an attractive glass serving bowl. Top with half the fruit mixture.

4 Repeat with another layer of yogurt and fruits and, finally, top with the remaining yogurt.

5 Place the walnuts in a small food processor and pulse until they are chopped into quite small pieces but not finely ground. Alternatively, chop them with a sharp knife. Sprinkle the walnuts over the top of the yogurt.

6 Drizzle the honey over the nuts and yogurt. Cover with plastic wrap and let chill in the refrigerator for at least 1 hour. Decorate the bowl with a small bunch of fresh red currants, if desired, just before serving.

lemon & lime syllabub

serves four

¼ cup superfine sugar

grated rind and juice of
 1 small lemon

grated rind and juice of 1 small lime

4 tbsp Marsala or
 medium sherry

1¼ cups heavy cream

lime and lemon rind, to decorate

NUTRITION

Calories 403	Sugars 16g
Protein 2g	Fat 36g
Carbohydrate 16g	Saturates 22g

1 Place the sugar, citrus juices and rind, and Marsala in a bowl, then mix well and let infuse for 2 hours.

2 Add the cream to the mixture and whisk until it just holds its shape.

3 Spoon the mixture into 4 tall serving glasses and let chill in the refrigerator for 2 hours.

4 Decorate with lime and lemon rind and serve.

COOK'S TIP

Do not overwhip the cream when adding it to the lemon and lime mixture, or it may curdle. Replace the heavy cream with lowfat plain yogurt for a lighter, healthier version of this dessert, or alternatively, use half quantities of both yogurt and cream. Whip the cream before adding it to the yogurt.

VARIATION

For an alternative citrus flavor, substitute 2 oranges for the lemon and lime, if you prefer.

lime mousse with mango

serves four

generous 1 cup mascarpone cheese

grated rind of 1 lime

1 tbsp superfine sugar

½ cup heavy cream

MANGO SAUCE

1 mango

juice of 1 lime

4 tsp superfine sugar

TO DECORATE

4 cape gooseberries

strips of lime rind

NUTRITION

Calories 254	Sugars 17g
Protein 5g	Fat 19g
Carbohydrate 17g	Saturates 12g

COOK'S TIP

Cape gooseberries have a tart and mildly scented flavor and make an excellent decoration for many desserts. Peel back the papery husks to expose the bright orange fruits.

1 Place the mascarpone cheese, lime rind, and sugar in a large bowl and mix together.

2 Whip the cream in a separate bowl and fold into the mixture.

3 Line 4 decorative molds or ramekin dishes with cheesecloth or plastic wrap and divide the mixture evenly between them. Fold the cheesecloth or plastic wrap over the top and press down firmly. Let chill in the refrigerator for 30 minutes.

4 To make the sauce, slice through the mango on each side of the large flat pit, then cut the flesh from the pit. Remove the skin.

5 Cut off 12 thin slices of mango and reserve. Chop the remaining mango and place in a food processor or blender with the lime juice and sugar. Blend until smooth. Alternatively, push the mango through a strainer, then mix with the lime juice and sugar.

6 Turn the molds out onto serving plates. Arrange 3 slices of mango on each plate and pour some sauce around, then decorate and serve.

melon & kiwifruit salad

serves four

½ Galia melon

2 kiwifruit

4½ oz/125 g white seedless grapes

1 papaya, halved

3 tbsp orange-flavored liqueur, such
  as Cointreau

1 tbsp chopped fresh lemon
  verbena, lemon balm, or mint

TO DECORATE

fresh lemon verbena sprigs

cape gooseberries

NUTRITION

Calories 88	Sugars 17g
Protein 1g	Fat 0.2g
Carbohydrate 17g	Saturates 0g

1 Remove the seeds from the melon and cut it into 4 slices, then carefully cut away the skin. Cut the flesh into cubes and place in a bowl.

2 Peel the kiwifruit and slice widthwise. Add to the melon with the grapes.

3 Remove the seeds from the papaya and discard and cut off the skin. Slice the flesh thickly and cut into diagonal pieces. Add to the fruit bowl and mix well.

4 Mix the liqueur and the chopped lemon verbena together, then pour over the fruits and let macerate for 1 hour, stirring occasionally.

5 Spoon the fruit salad into glasses and pour over the juices, then decorate with lemon verbena sprigs and cape gooseberries.

COOK'S TIP

Lemon balm or sweet balm is a fragrant lemon-scented plant with slightly hairy serrated leaves and a pronounced lemon flavor. Lemon verbena can also be used—this has an even stronger lemon flavor and smooth elongated leaves.

mini frangipane tartlets with lime

makes twelve

scant 1 cup all-purpose flour, plus
    extra for dusting
generous ¾ stick butter, softened
1 tsp grated lime rind
1 tbsp lime juice
¼ cup superfine sugar
1 egg
¼ cup ground almonds
¼ cup confectioners' sugar, sifted
½ tbsp water

1 Preheat the oven to 400°F/200°C. Reserve 5 teaspoons of the flour and 3 teaspoons of the butter.

2 Cut the remaining butter into the remaining flour until the mixture resembles fine bread crumbs. Stir in the lime rind, followed by the lime juice, then bring the mixture together with your fingers to form a soft dough.

3 Roll out the dough thinly on a floured counter. Stamp out 12 circles, 3 inches/7.5 cm wide, with a fluted cutter, and line a tartlet pan.

4 Cream the reserved butter and the superfine sugar together in a large bowl.

5 Mix in the egg, then the ground almonds and the reserved flour.

6 Divide the almond mixture between the pastry shells.

7 Bake in the preheated oven for 15 minutes, or until set and lightly golden. Turn the tartlets out onto a wire rack to cool.

8 Mix the confectioners' sugar with the water. Drizzle a little of the frosting over each tartlet and serve.

NUTRITION	
Calories 149	Sugars 9g
Protein 2g	Fat 9g
Carbohydrate 17g	Saturates 5g

pink syllabubs

serves two

5 tbsp white wine

2–3 tsp black currant liqueur

finely grated rind of ½ lemon

   or orange

1 tbsp superfine sugar

generous ¾ cup heavy cream

TO DECORATE

fresh fruits, such as strawberries,

   raspberries, or red currants, or

   pecan or walnut halves

fresh mint sprigs

NUTRITION

Calories 536	Sugars 17g
Protein 2g	Fat 48g
Carbohydrate 17g	Saturates 30g

COOK'S TIP

These syllabubs will keep in the refrigerator for 48 hours, so it is worth making more than you need and keeping the extra for another day.

1 Mix the wine, black currant liqueur, lemon rind, and sugar together in a bowl and let stand for at least 30 minutes.

2 Add the cream to the wine mixture and whip until the mixture has thickened enough to stand in soft peaks.

3 For a decorative effect, place the mixture into a pastry bag fitted with a large star or plain tip and pipe into 2 glasses. Alternatively, simply pour the syllabub into the glasses. Chill in the refrigerator until ready to serve.

4 Before serving, decorate each syllabub with slices or small pieces of fresh soft fruits or nuts and mint sprigs.

poached allspice pears

serves four

4 large ripe pears

1¼ cups orange juice

2 tsp ground allspice

⅓ cup raisins

2 tbsp brown sugar

grated orange rind, to decorate

COOK'S TIP

The Chinese do not usually have desserts to finish off a meal, except at banquets and special occasions. Sweet dishes are usually served in between main meals as snacks, but fruit is refreshing at the end of a big meal.

1 Using an apple corer, core the pears. Using a sharp knife, peel the pears and cut them in half.

2 Place the pear halves in a large heavy-bottom pan.

3 Add the orange juice, allspice, raisins, and sugar to the pan and heat gently, stirring, until the sugar has dissolved. Bring the mixture to a boil for 1 minute.

NUTRITION	
Calories 157	Sugars 17g
Protein 5g	Fat 19g
Carbohydrate 17g	Saturates 12g

4 Reduce the heat to low and let simmer for 10 minutes, or until the pears are cooked but still fairly firm—test them by inserting the tip of a small sharp knife.

5 Remove the cooked pears from the pan with a slotted spoon and transfer to serving plates. Decorate with the grated orange rind and serve hot with the syrup.

chocolate cheese pots

serves four

1¼ cups lowfat cream cheese

⅔ cup lowfat plain yogurt

2 tbsp confectioners' sugar

4 tsp lowfat drinking
    chocolate powder

4 tsp unsweetened cocoa

1 tsp vanilla extract

2 tbsp dark rum (optional)

2 egg whites

4 chocolate cake decorations,
    to decorate

assorted fruits, such as pieces of
    kiwifruit, orange, and banana,
    strawberries, and raspberries

NUTRITION

Calories 117	Sugars 17g
Protein 9g	Fat 1g
Carbohydrate 18g	Saturates 1g

1 Mix the cream cheese and yogurt together in a bowl. Sift in the sugar, drinking chocolate, and cocoa and mix well. Add the vanilla extract and rum, if using.

2 Whisk the egg whites in a clean bowl until stiff. Using a metal spoon, gently fold the egg whites into the chocolate mixture.

3 Spoon the cream cheese and chocolate mixture into 4 small china dessert pots and let chill in the refrigerator for 30 minutes.

4 Decorate each chocolate cheese pot with a chocolate decoration and serve with an assortment of fresh fruits, such as kiwifruit, orange, banana, strawberries, and raspberries.

COOK'S TIP

This would make a great filling for a cheesecake. Make the base out of crushed amaretti cookies and egg white. Set the filling with 2 tablespoons gelozone (vegetarian gelatin) dissolved in 2 tablespoons of boiling water.

pineapple with tequila & mint

serves four–six

1 ripe pineapple

sugar, to taste

juice of 1 lemon

2–3 tbsp tequila or a few drops of
vanilla extract

several fresh mint sprigs, leaves
removed and cut into thin strips

fresh mint sprig, to decorate

NUTRITION

Calories 87	Sugars 19g
Protein 1g	Fat 0g
Carbohydrate 19g	Saturates 0g

COOK'S TIP

Make sure you slice off the
"eyes" when removing the skin
from the pineapple.

1 Using a sharp knife, cut off the top and bottom of the pineapple. Place upright on a board, then slice off the skin, cutting downward. Cut in half, and remove the core if wished, then cut the flesh into chunks.

2 Place the pineapple in a bowl and sprinkle with the sugar, lemon juice, and tequila.

3 Toss the pineapple to coat well, then cover and let chill until ready to serve.

4 To serve, arrange on a large serving plate and sprinkle with the mint strips. Decorate the dish with a mint sprig.

VARIATION

Substitute 3 peeled sliced
mangoes for the pineapple. To
prepare mango, slice off a large
piece of flesh on either side of
the pit, then peel and cut into
chunks. Slice off the remaining
flesh attached to the pit.

raspberry fool

2 cups fresh raspberries

¼ cup confectioners' sugar

1¼ cups sour cream

½ tsp vanilla extract

2 egg whites

TO DECORATE

fresh raspberries

lemon balm leaves

NUTRITION

Calories 288	Sugars 19g
Protein 4g	Fat 22g
Carbohydrate 19g	Saturates 14g

COOK'S TIP

Although this dessert is best made with fresh raspberries, an acceptable result can be achieved with frozen raspberries, available from supermarkets.

1 Place the raspberries and sugar in a food processor or blender and process until smooth. Alternatively, press through a strainer with the back of a spoon.

2 Reserve 4 tablespoons of sour cream for decorating.

3 Place the vanilla extract and remaining sour cream in a bowl and stir in the raspberry mixture.

4 Whisk the egg whites in a separate mixing bowl until stiff peaks form. Gently fold the egg whites into the raspberry mixture using a metal spoon, until fully incorporated.

5 Spoon the raspberry fool into serving dishes and let chill for at least 1 hour. Decorate with the reserved sour cream, raspberries, and lemon balm leaves and serve.